# THE
# EMPATHETIC
# WORKPLACE

## KATHARINE MANNING

HarperCollins
LEADERSHIP

AN IMPRINT OF HarperCollins

*For my family.*
*Everything I am and everything I have*
*is because of you.*

Published by HarperCollins Leadership, an imprint of HarperCollins Focus LLC.

Any internet addresses, phone numbers, or company or product information printed in this book are offered as a resource and are not intended in any way to be or to imply an endorsement by HarperCollins Leadership, nor does HarperCollins Leadership vouch for the existence, content, or services of these sites, phone numbers, companies, or products beyond the life of this book.

ISBN 978-1-4002-2003-8 (eBook)
ISBN 978-1-4002-2002-1 (PBK)

Library of Congress Control Number: 2020949808

Printed in the United States of America
20 21 22 23 LSC 10 9 8 7 6 5 4 3 2 1

# Contents

# INTRODUCTION

Could a greater miracle take place than for us
to look through each other's eye for an instant?
— HENRY DAVID THOREAU

# An Empathetic Approach

L ife is messy. We strive for order. We set our goals and tick off our action items. We weigh our options and try to make good decisions. Nonetheless, the unexpected intervenes. We are knocked off track by challenges from the small to the life-changing: illness, accidents, bias, harassment, violence, financial woes, and more.

As much as we seek to avoid it, we carry these struggles with us. They affect us in our homes, in our communities, and they affect us at work. How leaders respond to the traumas that inevitably show up in their workplaces can determine the success or failure of the organization as a whole. An empathetic response instills trust, which in turn increases productivity, reduces absenteeism and turnover, and enhances engagement and satisfaction. Just as importantly, compassion makes it more likely that those in need will get help. It also bears noting that empathy lapses have shown up in more headlines and lawsuits than many would care to recount. This book teaches the skills to respond with calm and confidence to traumas at work, whenever and wherever they arise.

**BENTON SAT AT** the head of the table, with twenty sets of eyes fixed on him.[1] Arrayed around him were the mayor, the chief of police, the superintendent of schools, and other city leaders, each of whom had a deputy, who sometimes had a deputy.

Benton had been called to this room because of a tragedy. The city, like too many others before and after it, had experienced a school shooting. Now, headlines blared, news crews jostled for position in their formerly quiet town, and the streets were flooded with donations of flowers, toys, and cards from well-wishers. The nation grieved with them. But the city's leaders were paralyzed.

They needed a plan for ongoing support of the victims' families. They needed to decide when—or even whether—to reopen the school. They needed to answer the angry inquiries and threats of lawsuits about school security. And they needed to find a place for all of those donations.

The problem wasn't a lack of support. The federal government had offered them a near-blank check, as well as all the technical assistance and guidance they could need. The problem was that they couldn't act. Devastated by what had happened and overwhelmed by the hordes of outside press, donations, and aid, they had grown wary of offers of help and had developed the mind-set of a town under siege. Meanwhile, the school remained closed, no path for ongoing counseling had been established, and flowers wilted in the streets.

That was why Benton was here. Experienced in city crises from urban riots to a raid on a fundamentalist cult, Benton had been asked to come to this town to see if he could help break the impasse so that outside services could be brought in. Benton knew that logic, charts, plans of action, or statistics would not help.

Instead, he asked questions.

He asked about what had happened, and what had happened next, and what had happened after that. He asked about their roles, their thoughts, their regrets.

And as he asked, the tears began to flow. These civic leaders, in their gray suits with their padfolios, sat around that giant oak table and they wept. Benton, who had sat with mothers who had lost both sons to gang violence, with those who had been beaten and sexually assaulted, had never before seen so many tears in one room.

What those tears broke through was not an administrative logjam. It was the anguish at losing those beautiful children. It was the frustration at their own powerlessness. It was the devastating knowledge that this had happened on their watch. And because it broke through those, the administrative challenges were surmountable.

When the tears subsided, the mayor looked at Benton. "Clearly," he said, "we should have brought you in a long time ago."

I'VE BEEN WORKING with victims for more than twenty-five years as a counselor, advocate, and legal advisor. For fifteen years, I served as a senior attorney advisor with the Executive Office for United States Attorneys, advising the Justice Department on its most challenging victim issues in cases ranging from terrorism to large-scale financial fraud to child exploitation. Some of the cases I advised on include the Boston Marathon bombing, the Pulse nightclub and South Carolina church shootings, Charlottesville, Enron, Madoff, 9/11, and the federal case against Larry Nassar, doctor for the US Women's Olympic Gymnastics team. I have trained thousands of individuals on compliance with their responsibilities to victims, and I teach a course on victim rights at American University.

Through all of this work with diverse types of trauma, I began to realize something: all trauma is fundamentally the same. The degree varies, of course, and each person's experience is unique. The skills I would use to assist a victim of domestic violence on a hotline call, though, are the same ones I would use to comfort a colleague who bursts into tears in my office when one more assignment becomes one assignment too many or one who paces in front of my desk in anger at being belittled in a meeting. When the crisis comes—and all of us are going to face the crisis eventually—we need the same things.

Unfortunately, a lot of us struggle to give those things. We feel that we should have something more or different to give. We want to fix the problem.

We feel uncomfortable, for reasons that may be beyond our control (empathy can wreak havoc sometimes). It's messy and we don't want to get involved. Of course, by pushing these issues away, we only exacerbate them. They simmer below the surface, and eventually boil over. These issues are more prevalent than you might think.

# The Impact of Trauma at Work

Trauma is not a jacket that we can shed when we walk through the office door. We carry it with us. It affects our relationships, our physical and mental health, and it affects us at work. From sexual harassment and domestic violence to addiction and financial distress, the issues we face outside work come with us to work.

## How Trauma Appears in the Workplace

A survey of full-time employees found that 21 percent reported that they were victims of domestic violence. Of those, 74 percent had been harassed at work.[1] Workplaces can be dangerous for victims of domestic violence because even those who have managed to leave their abusers and go into hiding can always be found where they work. This makes our workplaces especially dangerous for those who are victims of domestic violence—and for everyone who works with them. Frighteningly, the majority of mass shootings in the United States are linked to domestic violence.[2] Even beyond the physical threat created by abusers who may come into the workplace, there are financial costs of domestic violence as well. The Department of Labor reports that victims of domestic violence lose nearly eight million days of paid work per year in the United States, resulting in a $1.8 billion loss in productivity for employers.[3]

Thirty-eight percent of women have been sexually harassed at work. This includes verbal, physical, and cyber harassment, as well as sexual assault.[4] Those who have been sexually harassed suffer long-term physical and mental health effects, including depression, high blood pressure, sleep disturbances, and a greater risk for posttraumatic stress disorder, as well as career limitations including lessened access to training and leadership opportunities as they attempt to avoid the harasser.[5] In addition to harming the victim of harassment, sexual harassment harms the organizations where it occurs. Teams in which sexual harassment occurs lose an average of $27,000 in productivity per team member—note that the loss in productivity goes beyond only the harassed and the harasser.[6] Harassment also leads to high turnover. Women who have experienced sexual harassment are six and a half times more likely to leave their jobs than those who have not.[7] Costs related to employee turnover are the highest cost of sexual harassment—considerably higher than the costs of litigation.[8]

African Americans are 60 percent more likely to experience discrimination than whites, and women are 53 percent more likely to experience discrimination than men.[9] One in four Black women has experienced discrimination at work.[10] Those who face bias against them are nearly three times more likely to be disengaged at work, more than three times as likely to be planning to leave their jobs, and two and a half times as likely to say that they've withheld ideas or solutions at work within the previous six months.[11]

Sexual assault can also impact the office. Current statistics show that one in five women, and one in fourteen men, are survivors of rape or attempted rape.[12] Sadly, half of sexual assault survivors lose or quit their jobs within one year of the assault, due to the severity of their trauma following the assault.[13] Even if they stay, survivors reported that their work was affected for up to eight months after the rape.[14]

Further, in a recent year, more than 2.5 million Americans lost money in a scam or other fraud, at a total cost of $1.7 billion.[15] Can financial abuse lead to trauma? Absolutely. From my time with the Justice Department, one of the stories that has stayed with me the longest is that of a woman in her seventies with multiple sclerosis, who had turned over her life savings to her minister in what turned out to be a Ponzi scheme. Homeless, she had resorted to sleeping on a friend's couch, with no prospects for her financial well-being. Over and over, I heard stories of bankruptcy, divorce, and suicides due to financial loss.

In 2018, more than fourteen million people were victims of identity theft.[16] On average, it takes about two hundred hours to recover from identity theft.[17] One in three victims of identity theft reported subsequent problems at work—not surprising, considering that the work of remediating bad credit and bounced checks largely must be done during working hours.[18] Twenty-two percent needed time off work to deal with the effects of the fraud, and 6 percent lost their jobs.[19]

The Centers for Disease Control and Prevention reports that six in ten adults in the United States suffer from a chronic illness, and four in ten have two or more illnesses.[20] In addition to the personal illnesses of workers, caregiving places a tremendous financial, physical, and emotional strain on families. Nearly 20 percent of retirees left the workplace earlier than they had planned due to the need to care for an aging spouse or family member.[21] According to the AARP, businesses in the United States lose an estimated $33.6 billion per year in productivity due to workers' caregiving responsibilities.[22] One can anticipate that these impacts will only increase as we face the fallout from the coronavirus.

The National Safety Council reports that more than twenty thousand assaults at work resulted in injury or illness in 2018, with an average of five days subsequently lost from work.[23] A person a day is shot at work.[24] A study of emergency room nurses found that 94 percent of those who had been assaulted at work suffered at least one symptom of posttraumatic stress disorder (PTSD), and 17 percent had enough symptoms to make it likely that they suffered from PTSD.[25] Thirty-seven percent demonstrated a decrease in productivity following the violent event.[26]

The fact is, if we work with people, we are working with people in trauma.

Lost productivity, absenteeism, and turnover are the quieter, and thus more insidious, costs. They can affect our organizations for generations without leadership even knowing that they exist. Some costs are noisier, though. They come in with a bang—with headlines and subpoenas. As countless companies and educational institutions can attest, a high-profile claim of sexual harassment, assault, or discrimination can devastate your organization's financial health and workplace culture. The *New York Times* reported in 2018 that in the year after the #MeToo Movement shot through the culture, more than two hundred prominent men lost their jobs due to accusations of assault and harassment, in claims brought by nearly a thousand people.[27] The companies they led often faced devastating impacts due to their misconduct.

These include the Weinstein Company, which filed for Chapter 11 bankruptcy months after news stories revealed the decades of sexual harassment, assault, and rape committed by joint founder and chief executive Harvey Weinstein.[28] Share prices in clothing company Guess dropped 18 percent in the hours after its cofounder Paul Marciano was publicly accused of sexual harassment—a loss of $250 million in market value in one day.[29] When the *Wall Street Journal* reported on multiple claims of sexual harassment brought against Steve Wynn, founder and CEO of Wynn Resorts, the company lost $3.5 billion in value. Wynn himself lost $412 million of his personal net worth.[30] Fox News reported in 2017 that it had paid more than $45 million in litigation costs associated with harassment claims.[31] The University of Southern California settled for $215 million in a class action suit with patients of a campus gynecologist who'd committed sexual misconduct.[32]

If we can catch these impacts when they're still in the quiet phase, we stand a better chance of heading them off before they get to the noisy phase. A better response to trauma will also change your workplace. If companies can uncover these issues before they blow up in spectacular fashion, they will create workplaces that are more productive, with lower rates of absenteeism and turnover. A healthy work environment is one where issues are not permitted to fester. To create such an environment, we must make it permissible to talk about the issues that are troubling us, whether those issues arise in the workplace or not.

## Trust: The Holy Grail of Workplace Culture

One CEO told me about an employee who was underperforming. He'd always been a good worker. His supervisors knew his wife was sick, but that didn't seem to account for his performance issues, which were abysmal—showing up late, not turning in work, zoning out in meetings. There was talk of firing him. Instead, someone from the management team took him aside and asked, "What's going on?" Though the employee had been loath to discuss his problems, once he was asked, it all poured out. His wife was much sicker than he'd told them. He was caring for her at night, taking her to doctor's appointments early in the morning, and trying to keep up with all the bills. In addition, the emotional weight of her illness was overwhelming. He was afraid he was going to lose her. Once those around him understood the extent of the burden he was carrying outside work, they were able to put some temporary supports around him. The employee was so grateful, as the CEO put it, "his performance did a 180."

I'm not surprised. By opening up a conversation with this employee during a difficult personal time, the company's leadership demonstrated that they cared about him beyond his temporary performance issues. Through this show of support, the company's leadership earned his trust.

Trust in the workplace is the holy grail when it comes to achieving a healthy and productive workforce. When employees trust their management, companies are rewarded with higher effort and performance, greater employee satisfaction and citizenship behavior, collaboration and teamwork, strategic alliances, and better responses to organizational change.[33] As Doug Conant, the former CEO of Campbell's Soup, puts it, "[Trust] is the foundational element of high-performing organizations." When he took the helm at Campbell's, Conant made "Inspiring Trust" his first mission in turning around the company's performance, which eventually led to shareholder returns in the top tier of the global food market and among the highest levels of employee engagement in the Fortune 500.[34] The Great Place to Work Institute has found that "trust between managers and employees is the primary defining characteristic of the very best workplaces."[35] In fact, employees who displayed a high degree of trust in their management, compared with lower-trust companies, had 74 percent less stress, 106 percent more energy at work, 50 percent higher productivity, 13 percent fewer sick days, 76 percent more engagement, 29 percent more satisfaction with their lives, and 40 percent less burnout.[36]

## Flushing Out Problems

One way to build and maintain trust in a workforce is through standing by it in difficult moments. You can't provide help if you don't know that something is a problem. That's why it's essential to cultivate a work environment in which it is acceptable to discuss hard issues, and ensure that when someone does come forward to share something difficult, he is met with a helpful response.

Flushing out these issues also allows us to address them. People tend to minimize bad behavior directed at them and many are reluctant to bring forward complaints, for a host of reasons ranging from not wanting to be seen as a victim or a troublemaker to humiliation to fear of reprisal. The US Equal Employment Opportunity Commission estimates that 75 percent of individuals who are harassed at work do not file a complaint.[37] If one person has identified a problem in the workplace, chances are it has been a problem for others as well.

Jessica[38] was the person in her office designated to receive complaints of sexual harassment, but she didn't even recognize it when it happened to her. She began a new project with a man she'd known around the office for a few years. After a few months of working together, he began sending her offensive text messages. He was older than she was, and she thought perhaps he was misreading social cues, or that he didn't realize how his messages came across. Not wanting to make a fuss, she took him aside privately and said, "You really can't send messages like this. They're creepy." It was only months later when another colleague made a formal complaint to her about the texts the colleague had been receiving from the same guy that the light clicked on for Jessica. Her colleague had actually been harassing her, and she wasn't the only one. An investigation revealed that he'd been sending similar texts to dozens of women in the office, for years.

Abusers are generally serial abusers. Numerous studies of college and military men have found that anywhere from 4 to 16 percent of men have committed a rape, and of those, two-thirds have raped multiple times (an average of four times in a single year of college), accounting for approximately 90 percent of rapes.[39] It's really Not All Men. It's a small number of serial abusers.

Thus, when someone comes forward to disclose assault or harassment in the workplace, there is a good possibility that numerous other people are suffering from the same abuse but haven't reported it. We should therefore celebrate those who come forward. They are alerting us to a problem that is likely affecting others and has an impact on productivity, absenteeism, and turnover. We cannot address the things we cannot see. Those who help us to see are doing us a service.

# The LASER Method

How can we encourage people to come forward? One way is by ensuring that when they do come forward, the response they get is respectful and supportive. An essential first step to an open environment, a workplace where difficult issues can be discussed without fear and handled without discomfort, is a good response when those issues are raised. This is both simpler and more difficult than it seems. Trauma impacts the brain of both the speaker and the listener. As discussed in the next chapter, adrenaline surges through our bodies and can make it hard to stay present and supportive.

What we need to do to support someone in trauma, however, is not complex. There are five steps, each of which is discussed in detail in this book.

# Listen

Active listening involves more than keeping your mouth shut. Controlling your own reaction, managing your body language, asking open-ended questions, hearing what is not being said, and winding down the speaker when the conversation becomes unproductive are essential elements of being a good listener. Step One covers all of these, plus how to prepare for a difficult conversation, take notes without interrupting the flow of conversation, and handle special circumstances involving mandatory reporting and threats of self-harm or harm of others.

# Acknowledge

Once someone shares a difficult personal story with you, it is important to acknowledge that gift. This is a brief moment that separates the speaker's recitation of a difficult story and your moment to begin talking. When acknowledging, we should mirror the speaker's language, speak with sincerity, and avoid distancing assumptions. This section of the book also provides tips on appropriate acknowledgments (and those that aren't so great).

# Share

One of the most difficult aspects of victimization is the loss of control. You can help the speaker regain some measure of control by sharing information with him or her. Though you may be limited in what you can share by the need for confidentiality or because you do not in fact know what happened, this step discusses the four types of information that can be shared: process, values, facts, and what you don't know, but hope to learn. It also discusses apologies.

# Empower

This step is equally important for the speaker and the listener. The traumatized person is going to have to continue on his journey without you. You can help that person by providing him with resources. Step Four details sample resources and gives advice on the types of services of which managers and others responsible for employees or members of the public should be aware. It also includes a caution against the common urge to take over next steps for the speaker; instead, we should let the person in trauma chart his own course.

# Return

The final step is to ensure that the injured person has a way to come back later, when he or she cannot remember all that you said, thinks of more questions, or wishes for updates. To leave matters on a solid footing, it is worthwhile to give the speaker a way to reach you again, whether this is a simple "call anytime," an email address, or a website where updates will be posted. "Return" is also a return to ourselves, and so this section includes information on compassion fatigue and self-care.

**THE STEPS ARE** thus: Listen. Acknowledge. Share. Empower. Return. They can be remembered in the moment when adrenaline floods our brains with their simple acronym: LASER. The goal is to help you stay focused (laser focused) on what needs to happen in that interaction to support the person who is experiencing something challenging. The LASER technique can benefit all who are responsible for others, from top-tier managers at Fortune 500 companies to residence advisors in college dormitories.

Throughout the book, and in particular at the start of each section of the LASER process, there are stories of those who have undergone trauma in one form or another. I generally believe that survivors should be able to tell their own stories. I have included these stories here because I think it's helpful to illuminate what works and doesn't work when interacting with those in trauma. Where possible, I have received permission from those whose stories I've included to retell them here. Where it is not possible, I have changed details and masked identities to protect people's privacy.

Some may be reluctant to encourage people to share difficult stories in the workplace, believing that these types of stories of trauma have no place in the office. They reason that encouraging people to come forward to talk about challenges at home, sick relatives, or bullying by coworkers will only detract from the work that needs to be done, and that we have far too much to do to spend our time hashing out personal issues. Thus, they argue that it is best to encourage a clear separation between work and home—and personal problems should be left at home.

But as Robert Frost says, "No way out but through." Ignoring a problem doesn't make it go away. It'll continue to dog you—in performance issues, absenteeism, attrition—and one day may rear its head in a spectacular fashion. The time you take to address these issues today pays off down the line.

A supportive response also does not necessarily take longer than an unsupportive one. The goal is not long and involved conversations, it's creating the appropriate response the first time, so that tension doesn't simmer and issues can be dealt with quickly. Later in the book, you'll find advice on how to lower the stress in the room, how to streamline the conversation by understanding what's driving it that is *not* being said, and how to wind up the discussion gracefully when it is no longer productive.

The LASER approach is not counseling. The goal of the LASER technique is not to help people in trauma heal from the effects of the trauma, to change the way they view something that happened to them, or to uncover long-buried hurts. The goal is simply to remain present while individuals share something difficult, and to give them the information and resources they need to continue on their way. It aims to give you the tools to participate in that conversation in a way that is helpful, and that doesn't harm the person in the trauma or get your organization into trouble.

You are not there to guide individuals in trauma through their long recovery. They need to find their own advocates and healing methods. Healing from trauma can be a long-term endeavor; it can take months or even years. This book is much narrower in scope. It is aimed at the moment when a survivor shares her story, and details how to respond appropriately so that you aren't creating more damage and you leave open the possibility that the survivor can get support. Later in the book, I will share resources with you that you can share with the survivor. These resources will help the survivor to take further steps on her own and continue along the path to healing.[1]

The LASER approach is also not crisis communications. Crisis communications refers to the method for communicating a public response to a difficult event. LASER is instead focused on responding to those who have themselves suffered harm. As an example, imagine that a gunman enters a retail store and begins firing. The store's communication with the press and public about what happened, its next steps, and what safety measures it has in place would be crisis communications. LASER instead focuses on the store's communications with those hurt—its employees and customers who were present during the shooting, those who may be afraid to come into the store, and neighboring stores that were affected by the shooting. While the information in this book may be helpful in formulating a public response (for instance, the section on sharing information may have important lessons for those contemplating communications with the public after a challenging event), its aim is not the public but rather the individuals or groups directly affected by a traumatic event.

In addition, though I am a lawyer and the law is the lens through which I view many situations, this book does not provide legal advice. Some sections, most particularly the section on apologies, will touch on legal issues and the ramifications in litigation of different approaches. The ideas discussed are general considerations; for advice on particular matters where a legal perspective is needed, it would be wise to consult an attorney.

What this book will give you, instead, are the tools to handle with empathy, composure, and confidence crises that arise in the workplace. LASER will help you when an employee mentions that her ex-husband has been hanging around outside the building and she's a little nervous, or a longtime client tells you that he has terminal cancer, or a customer threatens "to come back here with a gun." It provides practical advice to help those who work with humans respond to issues that are uniquely human. It will help you navigate the hard times with strength and confidence. It will give you a plan.

# Trauma and the Brain

efore we move on to the five steps of LASER, it is important to understand a few things about why we sometimes struggle to remain supportive when hearing a story of trauma. Our responses are not always logical, and that's because of the way we're wired. This chapter discusses trauma's impact on the brain, both of the person experiencing trauma and of those interacting with him. This affects us all, as I was reminded recently.

I sat across from a friend at an outdoor café, sipping a cup of tea as she wrapped both hands around her large mug of cappuccino. "I'd like to ask your advice on something," she said. "My older brother sexually assaulted me when I was twelve years old. I have been through so much therapy—I'm okay now—but I've cut off all ties with him. I know that he has kids, including little girls. Is it my responsibility to speak out now, to protect them?"

I had been doing victim work for more than twenty-five years when I had this conversation. I had heard so many stories of horrible things that people have endured. I had sat with sexual assault survivors through flashbacks, when they saw their rapists coming at them and experienced a terrifying, visceral fear. I had been trained, had read extensively, and had taught others how to do this. And yet, my mind froze. I struggled to remind myself to stay present with my friend as my brain fought to reject the disclosure. I didn't want this to have happened to her. As I strained to unspool the proper words—*this was not your fault, and it's not your responsibility to save anyone else*—my thoughts battled against each other, with one side advocating a complete shutdown and denial of the information that had just been imparted and the other whispering, *Stay present for her, stay present for her.*

All those years of training couldn't save me from that reaction. They did allow me to recognize what was happening. To understand why we so often bobble the response when someone shares with us something upsetting, it is helpful to know a bit about trauma and the brain.[1]

## How Trauma Affects Us

When we are faced with danger, our brains work to protect us. Often, this means that we get a flood of adrenaline, in case we need to take some action. Those parts of our brains that are less helpful for immediate self-protection, like the part responsible for rational decision-making, are impaired. This response is automatic, and it kicks in anytime our brains determine that we are in danger, whether because an attacker is coming toward us or because we are facing down an audience of three hundred people waiting for us to enlighten them with our words. This means that when we are under stress, we may feel a rush of energy and have difficulty forming rational thoughts.[2]

The next thing to understand are mirror neurons.

Mirror neurons were first discovered by scientists studying the brain of the macaque monkey. Researchers were analyzing the parts of the monkeys' brains that lit up when they reached for something. Then, one day, the scientists took their lunch break in the lab, and something strange happened. When the monkeys saw the researchers reaching for their own food, the monkeys' brains lit up as if they themselves had reached for food.[3] The brain had the same reaction whether the monkey itself was reaching for the food or if it merely saw someone do it. Another study found that a rat that observes another in pain has the same brain response as if it had itself experienced the pain.[4]

Researchers believe this is related to our tendency to mimic the expressions, posture, body language, and speech patterns of those with whom we are interacting.[5] When we see someone having an experience that we can understand and relate to, our brains mirror the experience of the person we see. You have probably had the experience of seeing someone across the room laugh really hard. This causes you to smile, or to begin laughing yourself, even if you have no idea what they are laughing at. Similarly, imagine that you are watching a football game on television and one of the players takes a really rough hit. You wince, right? You are safe and sound and sitting on your couch, and yet you wince right along with him. This is our mirror neurons at work.

Mirror neurons appear to be connected to empathy. In scans, the part of the brain that reacts when seeing someone in pain (that wince reaction) is more active in those with high empathy and less active in those with psychopathy.[6] Scientists believe that the mirroring of painful experiences establishes "a matching of psychological states between the sufferer and the observer, which ultimately supports empathic understanding and motivate[s] prosocial action."[7] Or, as one of the authors of the rat study said, "Empathy, the ability to feel with the emotions of others, is deeply rooted in our evolution."[8]

Thus, when we see someone else experience stress, our stress levels tend to rise too. One study, for instance, paired up participants, with one undergoing a stressful experience (giving an ad hoc five-minute presentation or doing complex math problems) while another merely watched. Observers' stress levels (measured by cortisol levels and heart rate) increased along with the persons they observed. This was exacerbated when the two were intimate partners, but coordinated stress levels occurred even between strangers. Men and women showed no difference in their empathetic responses.[9]

There are benefits to emotional contagion. It helps us to understand other people better and makes us feel closer to them. This is a powerful way to build relationships. In terms of survival, seeing another experience stress and feeling that stress yourself may help motivate you to protect yourself from what the other person fears.[10]

Emotional contagion is thus hardwired into us and serves to protect us and connect us to others. We wouldn't want to get rid of it, and we couldn't if we tried. The key is to recognize its effect on us and learn to counterbalance it when necessary so that it doesn't thwart what we're trying to do.

## Managing the Effects of Trauma

If someone comes to tell you about a difficult event, that person is likely experiencing an elevated stress level. You may catch some of that stress, simply by observing. Here are some ways to recognize a stress response in yourself:[11]

A surge of anger
Clenched jaw
Desire to punch, stomp, or kick
A knotted or burning feeling in your stomach
Your voice raises
You glare at people
Restless legs
You fidget
You feel trapped
Numbness in your extremities
Your eyes dart around, looking for an exit
You feel leaden, dull
Your skin pales
Your heart rate decreases
Your heart pounds
You have a sense of dread

Again, these are normal responses that your highly functional brain sets into motion to protect you. They simply aren't helpful in the moment when someone comes to you for help, because they pull you out of the moment when you want to be present and supportive for the other person.

The first step to managing that response is to recognize it. *Ah, my heart is beating really fast. That's my stress response because this is a hard conversation.*

Or, *I'm having trouble processing what he's saying. I wonder if that's because I'm catching some of his distress.* Or, *I can't catch my breath. That's my body trying to pump more oxygen into my muscles in case I need to run.*

Just recognizing it will help you to get a handle on the reaction. You'll start to think something like, *Silly, really. Why would I need to run?* And that will begin to calm you. Employing some deliberate calming techniques will help even more. The goal is to remind yourself that you are fine. You're completely safe. Here are a few ideas:

- *Breathe.* Specifically, breathe intentionally and slowly. Breathe in for a count of four and out for a count of six. Notice your stomach expand as you breathe in and contract as you breathe out.
- *Engage the five senses.* Make note of the color of the walls, the smell of coffee from the break room next door, the sound of laughter down the hall, the feel of your watch on your arm. All of this will help bring you back to the present moment when you are not, in fact, being attacked by a bear but rather are sitting quietly at your desk.
- *Release the tension.* Find a nonobstructive way to let out some of the energy surging through you. Flex and release your calves or your fists. Curl your toes. Clench your stomach and then consciously let it go.
- *Focus on something calming.* This can be a phrase, something in the room, or even a memory. Think to yourself, over and over again, *I'm fine.* Glance at the photo on your desk of your spouse or child. Picture a candle or gentle waves on a peaceful ocean.
- *Double down on empathy.* Sometimes our stress response shows up as disbelief, anger, disgust, or a shutting down of emotion. Recognize that this is your body trying to protect you from feeling, and instead, lean the other way. Ask yourself, *How would I feel if this were me?* Or, *How would I feel if this were my sister?* Try to put yourself in the other person's shoes to bring yourself back to how that person is feeling and being present for him or her. This may be the most effective strategy of all, so long as you're not ignoring your own stress response, because it brings online brain systems involved

in caring and nurturing, which have the opposite biological impacts of those involved in fear and self-protection.

Use any of these, alone or in conjunction, when you notice your stress response kick in. This will help you to stay calm and focused during the conversation, rather than allowing yourself to be hijacked into an unnecessary stress reaction. Managing your own response will lower your stress level, which is a benefit on its own. Even better, your calm will be contagious and help the speaker to feel calmer as well. Finally, it will keep you focused on the person in front of you and what he or she needs, so that your response can be helpful and supportive.

It's also possible that you may feel none of these things. You may, in fact, feel nothing at all. Empathy varies widely from person to person and from situation to situation. Some things are really hard for me to hear, because of my own life experiences, my relationship with the speaker, or simply because of how the story strikes me on that day. Others aren't. And I know that I tend toward the more empathetic end of the spectrum. But lots of people do not, or they have trained the natural empathetic response out of themselves so as to respond in a way that seems more professional and deliberative. One's mileage varies, as they say, by disposition, situation, and day.

Empathy is not inherently good or bad. It just is. It allows us to feel connected to others, which can be great in some situations and problematic in others. The key is to recognize when it's needed, when we're feeling its effects, and how either to summon it or mitigate it depending on the situation.

# STEP ONE

## LISTEN

Courage is what it takes to stand up and speak;
courage is also what it takes to sit down and listen.
— WINSTON CHURCHILL

# Introduction

The first step in LASER is also the most important step. If we do nothing else, listening to those in trauma will make a tremendous difference in the person's healing and in demonstrating that it is okay to bring up challenging issues. Unfortunately, our instincts are often not to listen. Listening can be uncomfortable and thus often we communicate inadvertently that we want the speaker to cease talking. In this step of the LASER process, I will discuss why listening is so important, as well as how to listen, noticing and controlling our own response when someone is sharing a difficult story, and special circumstances like when we believe the person is lying or fear that the person is a danger to himself or others.

I was a sophomore in college when I first understood how difficult it is to hear a story of trauma. I'd recently begun volunteering at a domestic violence shelter on the hotline. Hotline calls are anonymous, but one caller had rung through often enough that I had gotten to know her a little. Let's call her

Jane. I had spoken to Jane as she left her abuser—no easy task, as part of the abuse is often isolating the victim from family and friends, controlling her finances, and crucially, destroying her self-esteem. Experts estimate that the average victim of domestic violence leaves seven times before finally breaking free for good.[1]

Jane had managed it, though. She left him, taking their six-year-old daughter. I shared her joy at the freedom she finally clutched in her bruised and shaky hands as she moved into her own apartment for the first time, and her frustration at the legal system as she wound her way through byzantine divorce proceedings without the aid of an attorney. To my shock, her abuser was awarded visitation with their daughter because, the court reasoned, the fact that he was abusive to his wife did not mean he was a bad father.[2]

Then one afternoon I picked up the hotline and was met with a sound unlike any I had ever heard in my life, before or since. It was a keening, animal wail, and it lasted long enough to pierce my skull and travel into my bones, where it resides to this day.

It was Jane.

She had just returned from the pediatrician's office, where she'd learned that the bruises and lacerations on her daughter's genitals were not playground injuries but rather were evidence of her ex-husband's molestation of their daughter, during court-ordered visitation. I was the first person she spoke to after discovering this.

I was nineteen years old.

I was not a lawyer or a doctor, nor a priest or police officer. I had no children and had never been married. I had no idea what to say to Jane. Instead, I had an overwhelming urge to put down the phone and go find someone else. Surely anyone would be better able to handle this than I.

There was, of course, no one else who could field this call. There was only me. Fortunately, that I had no advice for Jane meant that I was left with only one option, and it was the one thing Jane actually needed: I listened.

I gripped the phone to my ear—knuckles white, stomach turning—as she choked out her story and I murmured, again and again, "Oh, Jane, I am so sorry."

Eventually, the sobs lessened. Her words, still a jumble, came out in longer phrases.

"Oh, Jane, I am so sorry."

I sat with her in that moment, the very worst moment of her life—worse than the abuse she suffered at his hands for so many years, worse than the uptick in violence when she prepared to leave, worse than the terrifying prospect of her penniless future.

"Oh, Jane, I am so sorry."

With a few last, shuddering breaths, she stopped crying. "Okay," she said. "Okay." And then she hung up.

LISTENING IS NOT easy. The stories of trauma that we hear can stay with us, sometimes forever. They can impact our physical and mental health.[3] But at the same time, it is the greatest gift we can give. When we give survivors room to share their story, we aid in their healing and show respect for them and all they have gone through. On that hotline call so many years ago, what Jane needed was to release that pain so that she could go back and love her daughter, and fight for her. Which she did. She was a strong and fierce advocate, and I know her daughter is all right today because of Jane. It is worthwhile to stay present and listen. In this section, I will teach you how to do that.

# Why We Listen

W hy do people want to talk about difficult things, anyway? Discussing traumatic events has not always been seen as helpful. My grandfather fought at the Battle of the Bulge in World War II, where nearly one hundred thousand American troops were lost, wounded, or killed. When I tried to get him to talk about the war, he always demurred. At most, he would share stories of the pranks he and his fellow GIs would pull on each other. As was common for his generation, he saw no benefit to reliving painful memories.

It is perhaps the horrors of World War II, however, that led to a growing cultural understanding that some things are so horrific that they cannot be borne in silence. They must be recounted—to avoid the same horrors, yes, but also simply to know, and to be known. As Elie Wiesel said in his haunting memoir, *Night*, "For the dead and the living, we must bear witness." Though each individual's story, and his reasons for sharing it, are unique, there are a few common reasons that people speak out about a painful experience.

## Acknowledgment

For more than a decade, El Salvador was engulfed in a bloody civil war. To reckon with the violence that had so torn apart the country, the warring factions agreed to a United Nations Truth Commission. The Commission's mandate was to "investigat[e] serious acts of violence that have occurred since 1980 and whose impact on society urgently demands that the public should know the truth."[1]

Despite citizens' ongoing fear of reprisal, the Commission heard testimony from witness after witness on the atrocities of the war. As one commissioner noted, "For some, ten years or more had gone on in silence and pent-up anger. Finally, someone listened to them and there would be a record of what they had endured. They came by the thousands, still afraid and not a little skeptical, and they talked, many for the first time. One could not listen to them without recognizing that the mere act of telling what had happened was a healing emotional release, and that they were more interested in recounting their story and being heard than in retribution. It is as if they felt some shame that they had not dared to speak out before, and now that they had done so, they could go home and focus on the future less encumbered by the past."[2]

Recent protests against police brutality often include the rallying cry, "Say His Name." Literally, acknowledge that this person existed, and was lost. Sharing a story of trauma permits a validation of what the person experienced. When individuals can tell their story, and be heard and acknowledged, that can allow them a sense of dignity.

## Healing

Telling a story of trauma is often healing. A secret can be like a wound that aches and demands attention. Keeping secrets actually stresses our brains, as the prefrontal cortex, which controls our complex decision-making and thus thinks through potential negative outcomes and dangers, battles with our cingulate cortex, which wants to share information so that it can move on to more important tasks. The flood of stress hormones this causes can affect our sleep and have other negative physical effects.[3] Survivors who share their stories show lower rates of depression and posttraumatic stress than those who keep their stories secret.[4] Our own experiences have likely taught us the negative impact of harboring secrets, particularly long-term secrets.

To study the impact of sharing emotional pain, researchers gathered a group of healthy adults who were to undergo a biopsy. Before the surgery, half of the group was instructed to write a story about a painful experience. The other half was instructed to write out the story of a neutral experience. After the surgeries, the groups' rates of healing were compared. The study participants who wrote out a story of a traumatic event had significantly higher rates of healing compared with the second group.[5] Releasing a story of trauma is healing.

This has been so recognized by the medical community that many medical schools now have narrative medicine programs.[6] These programs help doctors to gain "the ability to listen to the narratives of the patient, grasp and honor their meanings, and be moved to act on the patient's behalf"—in effect, they are taught how to hear patients' stories to aid in their healing.[7]

The healing power of storytelling also led Ron Capps to create the Veterans' Writing Project. Capps, a military veteran of twenty-five years who witnessed genocide in Rwanda and Kosovo, has the words "Either you control the memory or the memory controls you" hanging in his office. Capps found that writing about his own experiences helped him to heal. When he teamed up with a research psychologist from the University of Texas, Austin, they learned that when college students wrote about their thoughts and feelings about a traumatic event for just fifteen minutes a day, four days in a row, they visited the health center fewer times over the next six months and reported a better mood, a more positive outlook, and greater physical health.[8]

An important part of healing from a traumatic event is the process of storytelling—the way that we shape what happened to us into a coherent narrative that fits in our lives and how we envision ourselves. The act of crafting the event into a story helps the survivor to make sense of what happened in their own minds and place it into the larger context of what they understand of who they are and how they have lived their lives. As Chanel Miller writes in her book, *Know My Name*, about her experiences following her assault by Stanford swimmer Brock Turner, "This is an attempt to transform the hurt inside myself, to confront a past, and find a way to live with and incorporate these memories."[9]

## Taking Control

Storytelling also allows us to seize back the narrative. Instead of the story being one of what happened to us, it becomes our story to tell, of our own experience. US Women's Olympic Gymnastics Team doctor Larry Nassar was prosecuted for multiple sexual assaults of those in his care. At his sentencing hearing, Judge Rosemarie Aquilina allowed 156 victims to provide victim impact statements. Over seven days of gripping and moving testimony, these women addressed the man who had abused them when they were young and powerless, thereby seizing control back.[10] They described their own experiences of Nassar's abuse and the difficulty in getting others to believe them. They appeared not as powerless children but as strong, united women. Rachel Denhollander, one of the survivors who addressed the court, said that while she hated the idea of having cameras in the courtroom recording all of their statements, "It was very important to make it as clear as possible to Larry Nassar that he was not in control anymore—and that we were coming out swinging."[11] Or as Kyle Stephens put it, addressing Nassar directly, "Perhaps you have figured it out by now, but little girls don't stay little forever. They grow into strong women who return to destroy your world."[12]

## Building Community

Sharing a story also builds and strengthens community. That was the true power of the #MeToo Movement—it showed those who had experienced sexual assault and harassment that they were not alone. When we are able to share our troubled histories with another and be supported through that, it fortifies us and also strengthens our bonds with one another.

One woman discovered the power of sharing her experience after her child was stillborn. As she told her story through live speaking events and blogging, her isolation diminished: "The more I reach out, the more people reach back. It's helped me build a community."[13] When we open up, we learn that the things we thought were unique to us are in reality shared by others.

## Enacting Change

Disclosing stories of trauma also makes communities stronger by allowing them to change bad behavior. If a community is unable to face atrocities, it is doomed to continue perpetuating them. Perhaps this is what motivated Kurt Werner Schaechter. Schaechter sued the French National Railroad Service for its complicity with the Nazis in transporting prisoners (including his parents) to the death camps. He filed suit for one euro plus an acknowledgment of the role they played. "I am doing this out of a responsibility to history," he says. "What distinguishes us from animals is our memory. Humanity cannot forget its history."[14] A strong motivator for many survivors to share their stories is to protect others.

There are thus tremendous benefits, both for individuals and for society as a whole, to talking about painful events. As discussed in Chapter Two, it also helps our organizations in flushing out problems and enhancing trust. In order to reap those benefits, it is important that we learn to listen to these stories.

# Before the Meeting

An important part of listening begins before the person even walks through the door. For someone to feel comfortable sharing information with you, you need to have set the groundwork of respect. In addition, your own ability to listen and respond appropriately will be enhanced by taking some steps ahead of time to prepare yourself for a difficult conversation.

## Create a Safe Environment

Chris Wilson is a psychologist who specializes in trauma. In that role, he often trains lawyers and law enforcement officers on how to interact and communicate with people who've experienced trauma. One of the things he teaches is that our brain is always mapping environments as either safe or threatening, as part of the brain's efforts to keep us safe. If nothing in the environment is consistent with a threat, that environment is mapped as safe. When we've been through something traumatic, however, our brains unconsciously tend to generalize our maps related to the trauma. What used to be mapped as safe becomes mapped as threatening. So the victim of domestic violence whose spouse calls at work and is verbally abusive suddenly maps any ringing of the phone at work to threat and feels anxious. The veteran who faced combat overseas and had to patrol farmers markets as part of his job now maps the market in his hometown to threat and avoids going with friends. In my own experience, a friend who was dying of cancer had fresh lavender in her room for her last weeks. Twenty years later, that smell still brings me back to that room and my dying friend. I walk into a spa and abruptly feel dizzy and like I might throw up.

Whenever we communicate with someone about their trauma, it's important to remember that while we may think we represent a map of safety, due to our position of authority or to the way we act or react in the moment, we may inadvertently get mapped to threat. If that happens, we increase the chances that the person who came to us for help will feel the desire to shut down or even leave. We can help avoid that by acting in ways that are consistent with safety. There are a few things that help with that:

- *Offer choices*. Being a victim is about having choice removed, so offering choice is consistent with a map of safety. "Would you like the door open or closed?" "Where would you like to sit?" "Would you like something to drink?" "We have coffee, tea, and water. What sounds good?" When we give choices, we demonstrate that the person has autonomy in our presence. We will not seek to impose our will upon her; she is safe here.
- *Be transparent about your own limits*. "Thanks so much for coming in. I'm looking forward to our talk. I do want to let you know that I've got an eleven o'clock meeting, but we've got a good chunk of time before then. So what's up?" "I'm glad to see you, but I have a memo I have to get out this afternoon, so we can either talk quickly now or schedule a longer time tomorrow."
- *Be consistent and act in predictable ways*. If you are a naturally energetic person, do your best to tone it down. Don't jump up or shout

out, "Hey! I just remembered something! Be right back." I also try to speak in an even, slow, and relatively low voice. I may sound a little like a smooth jazz DJ, but people have told me that my voice is very calming.

- *Mind your demeanor during the interaction.* Wilson talks about the difference between listening with "safe eyes" and "hard eyes." "Hard eyes" is the approach that indicates that, first and foremost, you have a job to do. It's not just in your eyes but also in your tone and your posture. Your demeanor says, "I am in work mode and I am gathering facts for an important purpose." "Safe eyes" is the approach you take when you see the humanity of the person in front of you. Yes, you have a job to do, but it's secondary to respecting the person before you.[1]

  For those who are engineers, lawyers, doctors, and others who focus on fact gathering, be aware that your default may be hard eyes. Even when you are open to hearing from the person and interested in what he says, your gaze may be shutting down the conversation. In fact, for some, just concentrating looks like hard eyes. Be aware of how you come across and practice listening with a nodding head, a concerned look, and expressions of empathy.

- *Avoid touching the person.* This is not instinctive for me; I like to hug, pat people on the arm, or put a hand on a shoulder. I do it to establish warmth and connection, and because I myself find it comforting. What I've learned is that while this can be soothing for some, for others it can be triggering. For someone who has been sexually assaulted, a part of the sexual assault may have been a grooming process where the assailant first put a hand on her shoulder, and then later on her back, and then waist, over time pushing further boundaries. It's impossible to know the background and experience of the person with whom you are interacting, and I never want to assume that touching is okay or to put someone in the position of having to explain to me that it is not. Instead, I try always to ask, "Can I give you a hug?" "Are you a hugger?" I ask in a way to make clear that either answer is fine.

Even the appropriateness of asking, though, will depend on the circumstances and relationship of the two people. For friends having a cup of coffee together, it is probably fine. For an older supervisor with a younger employee, it may not be. If you aren't sure, it's better to err on the side of avoiding touch. The goal is to put the person at ease, not to create anxiety or discomfort inadvertently.

# Prepare Yourself

Beyond the general tips on interacting with those in trauma, it's also helpful to ensure that you are prepared and in the right frame of mind for the conversation. Let's walk through a common scenario. You are a manager, and someone on your team emails and asks to meet with you. You go through the logistics of finding a time, and when you try to suss out what the meeting is for, she responds with a terse, "It's about a personal matter. I just wanted to make you aware of something."

At that point, you think through some common possibilities. Pregnancy? An ill family member? Is she herself sick? Going through a divorce? You probably aren't thinking domestic violence or sexual assault. Statistically, though, there is a decent chance of that coming up. Approximately one-third of people will be victims of some form of violence by an intimate partner during their lifetimes, and more than 40 percent of women experience sexual violence during their lifetimes, according to the Centers for Disease Control and Prevention.[2] Refresh yourself about the security options available at your company. Are there opportunities for counseling of any kind? As a manager, it is worthwhile to be well versed in the different resources your workplace offers its employees. If you aren't, find a time to brush up on those before the meeting. Step Four discusses some of the common resources managers and others who work with people should know.

Now it's almost time for the meeting. You are in the middle of another project when your calendar sends up a reminder. *Right*, you think. *Olivia wanted to talk about something. A personal thing.* Give yourself a minute here to transition out of the project you're working on and get into the mind-set to listen. You don't know what's walking through that door. If most of your brain is still immersed in your project, you won't be able to hear what Olivia is saying and respond effectively. Close down the project. Maybe go for a walk, get yourself a cup of water. Make sure that you are on time and in the right mental frame for a personal discussion when Olivia walks through that door.

Of course, you won't always have the luxury of time to prepare yourself before the meeting. Olivia may stick her head in your office and say, "Can I talk to you real quick? It's about something personal."

If you aren't in the right frame of mind or know that your attention will be occupied with a pending deadline, consider whether it may be best to put off the meeting. Better to tell Olivia that you're in the middle of something and set up another time than to go into a potentially difficult conversation only half present.

If that won't work, you'll need to act immediately to transition your thoughts so that you can become present where you are. Take a minute to close the file you're working on, turn your monitor to the side (or, even better, off) so that pop-up emails or calendar notices don't distract you. Put away your cell phone.[3] Note how long you have before your next appointment. Take a breath or two. Now: give Olivia your full attention.

# Active Listening

**Y**ou know how to listen, right?

Keep your mouth shut and let the other person talk. Is it really more complicated than that?

A bit.

The reality is that most people are pretty awful at listening. We interrupt. We segue into a topic we care more about. We check the clock. We barely hear what the person is saying because we are so eager for them to take a breath so that we can jump in with something we know about that very topic!

None of this is listening. While you may think that you are engaging in a back-and-forth, what you are doing is shutting down the speaker. In some cases, this is fine. If you're at a cocktail party and someone is droning on about something incredibly boring to you, go ahead and steer the conversation to a topic less mind-numbing. If the speaker is saying something racist or sexist, feel free to stop that train midcourse with an "Ew, is this going to be racist? Please just don't."

But when someone comes to you with something heavy and burdensome, a different approach is required. In those moments, you need to call on active listening.

Active listening doesn't mean walking around the room or jumping into the conversation to say your piece. Active listening means I am fully engaged in listening to you. My attention is not elsewhere. I am consciously present and striving to understand your meaning.

As discussed earlier, listening is especially hard when the subject is something traumatic. Listening is always hard, though. Most people speak at a rate of about 125 words per minute.[1] We can understand speech, though, at rates of up to 400 words per minute and beyond.[2] What do we do with all that extra time? We try to guess what the person is going to say next. We think about what we would do in a similar situation. We decide whether we think the person is honest and has a correct understanding. Our minds wander away. We think about what we'll have for dinner or what our spouse said the day before or the email that we forgot to answer.

Some of this may be fine. Without interrupting the flow of the other person, we can make a quick mental note of the email to make sure we respond later, then let it go. Return to the present moment and the speaker. Staying focused on the conversation allows you to see and hear a lot more than you will if your mind wanders; it allows you to be much more helpful. In addition, it's important to demonstrate your attention is fully on the speaker so that he doesn't feel dismissed. There are a few ways to help you stay engaged and to show the speaker that you care.

## Encouragement

When listening to someone, of course, you do not sit mute and immobile. A conversation must be a give-and-take, even when one person is talking and the other is listening. If you do not respond at all to what the person is saying, he will become uncomfortable and trail off. Encourage him to continue with brief statements or sounds along the lines of "Uh-huh," "Of course," "Got it," or "Wow." All of this should be gentle and quiet. Your goal is to encourage the speaker to continue with his story, not to pull focus onto yourself. Try to read the speaker to understand when he needs encouragement and when you can remain silent and let the story spin out.

## Eye Contact

Have you ever talked with someone at a party who kept looking past you to the door, to see who else is coming in? It's pretty clear what that person is paying attention to, and it isn't you. Eyes have been called the window to the soul, or the doorway to the heart—in short, where you focus is what you care about.

The quickest way to show someone that she has your attention is through eye contact. She can see that you aren't distracted by your phone or glancing at someone in the hall. She knows that you are engaged in what she has to say.

One quick caution, though, is that the appropriateness of eye contact varies culturally. In some cultures, eye contact is considered rude. It is helpful if you have a sense of whether this would apply to the speaker ahead of time, but if you don't know the cultural background of the speaker, ask directly if eye contact is uncomfortable, or try to read her cues. If she is refusing to make eye contact, it could be a signal that she is uncomfortable with it, and you should follow suit by keeping your eyes down. If this is the case, you may need to employ other tactics to demonstrate that you are listening.

## Mirroring

As discussed in Chapter Four, mirroring is a hardwired brain response. We often mirror a speaker subconsciously. You may have noticed on some occasions that you and someone to whom you are speaking both have your arms crossed, or are leaning on your hand in the same way. This is those mirror neurons at work again. We mimic the body language of a speaker when we are fully engaged in what the speaker is saying, which both helps us to immerse ourselves in the speaker's story (we are physically experiencing what he is experiencing) and demonstrates to the speaker that we are right there with him.

If you don't consciously use this technique already, watch yourself over the next week or so, and see if you are unconsciously mirroring those with whom you are in conversation. It can be pretty funny once you see it.

Mirroring is a wonderful way to establish rapport and comfort between people, which will help the speaker to open up to you. If you do too much of this deliberately, it can be creepy, but a subtle nod to it can create an ease in the conversation.

You can also use mirroring in the opposite direction. If the speaker is really tense—shoulders tight, jaw clenched, fists balled—consciously adopt a more relaxed stance. Lower your own shoulders, take a deep breath in and out, and release your stomach. This will both help you to stay calm in the situation, and may lead to the speaker taking similar actions, helping him to stay calm, as well. This can be a great way to lower the temperature of a heated conversation.

# Looping

This can feel awkward at first, but it is surprisingly effective. You merely repeat back what the person says to you, as close as possible to their exact words. For example:

> Mia: I'm just so frustrated. No matter what I do, he won't stop.
> You: Wow, I can hear how frustrated you are. No matter what you
>     do, he won't stop.

Or:

> Tom: I feel lost. I don't know what to do.
> You: It sounds like you really feel lost, and like you don't know what
>     to do.

All you've done is repeat words, and the response you get is often along the lines of a relieved, "Exactly!" You're showing the speaker that you are listening, and for someone in trauma, that can be incredibly healing.

You may not feel comfortable trying this for the first time when you encounter someone in a truly traumatic situation. Instead, try it out with a friend or family member who is upset about something minor, like a traffic jam. Once you see the results, you'll be more comfortable trying it in a more difficult encounter.

# Clarification

Seeking clarification can both show the speaker that you are listening and ensure that you aren't misunderstanding. Here's what that sounds like.

> Paul: I'm just really frustrated about the whole thing.
> You: When you say you're frustrated about the whole thing, do you mean this interaction with David?

That exchange invites Paul to say more about what frustrates him. It shows him that you have been listening, by reciting back his precise language and giving a neutral summation of what he has discussed with you. Using his exact word ("frustrated") ensures that you are not distorting what he is telling you ("frustrated" is not quite the same as "mad" or "upset") and shows him that you are listening carefully.

Note that the summation is not slanted in a way to make Paul feel that you are on his side, or alternatively, are not believing him or are already building a case against him. You aren't, for instance, saying, "You mean the horrible way David has been treating you," or "What you *claim* happened with David." Finally, the clarifying question is short. This is not the time for a long dissertation on what you've understood him to say. The point here is to make sure you understand and invite him to explain more.

# Ask Open-Ended Questions

Asking open-ended questions demonstrates that you want the speaker to keep talking and gives you information that you need. An open-ended question is one that doesn't readily lead to a yes or no answer, and it generally begins with "who," "what," "where," or "when." A few examples might include, "When did this start?" "Who else was there?" "Where did you go next?" and "What did he say then?" They also demonstrate to the speaker that you are listening and engaged in what's being said. As noted in an article in the *Harvard Business Review*, "Sitting there silently nodding does not provide sure evidence that a person is listening, but asking a good question tells the speaker the listener has not only heard what was said, but that they comprehended it well enough to want additional information."[3] These questions are also a great way to kick-start the conversation if the speaker seems to peter out or to get back on track if the speaker is heading off on a tangent.

A brief note about why questions: they can be great, but you need to be thoughtful about when to use them. A why question can really open up the conversation and get the speaker talking, or it can make the speaker believe that you are suspicious of what's being said. The difference between the two is largely dependent on your demeanor in asking the question and the relationship between you and the speaker. "Why did you do that?" for instance, can sound like an invitation for a lengthy self-examination or like a rebuke, depending on your tone, body language, and facial expression. A similar question, though less severe in its swings of interpretation, is, "Can you give me an example of that?"

These questions can be incredibly useful, provided that you can be completely open and curious in how you ask them. This requires you to have a good understanding of your own reactions to what the speaker is saying, and to the speaker himself. Are you suspicious? Has he said things before that you doubt? Is what he's saying far-fetched? If the answer to any of those questions is yes, then it will be exceedingly difficult to keep that note of suspicion out of your voice as you ask the why questions.

Further, the greater the power differential between you and the speaker, the greater impact that will have. That includes both your power within your institution (are you a colleague? Supervisor? A few steps up the ladder?) as well as societal power (differences in gender, race, class, ability, sexual orientation, and age). The speaker will be keenly aware of that power difference and will feel the suspicion more acutely—to the point that he may feel suspicion even if you genuinely aren't harboring any.

How will that affect the person? He will shut down. He will stop telling his story, and you will get no further information. Or, alternatively, he will double down. He will grow more adamant about what he is saying, but not in a helpful way—he will become more emphatic but without sharing additional information that would help you understand. The conversation will become less productive and more emotional.

Therefore, be cautious in how you approach why questions. If you know that you have some suspicion about what is being said, or if there is a power difference between you and the speaker, take particular care to express your question in an open and curious manner. Be mindful of your body language and tone. A rapid-fire question, asked with a furrowed brow while leaning across the desk toward the speaker, will likely not be helpful. Lean back and display an open stance. Consider an introductory, clarifying remark to the question, such as, "I am just asking so that I fully understand—why did you tell the person it was okay?" Or, "That's a completely normal response, but I want to make sure I have all the information about what was going on for you, so can you tell me why you decided to go home at that point?" Strive to maintain as neutral and open a tone as possible, with the aim of demonstrating that you are genuinely curious.

Finally, as you ask questions, watch the demeanor of the speaker. Our goal is to show interest, not give the third degree. We also don't want to give the impression that we are asking questions out of a prurient interest. If you are an investigator and will need to write a report on what has been disclosed to you, you will obviously have to ask enough questions to generate a complete picture. But if you are not required to report on this event later, you may not need all of the details. We also must always be mindful that sharing a story of trauma can be retraumatizing. Try to balance the need to show the person that you are open to listening with watching the person's demeanor and backing off when it appears that responding to questions is difficult. Offer to take a break if the person seems to need it.

# Body Language

Body language is, of course, as important or even more important than what you say. Some experts say that more than half of communication is done through body language.[4] Anyone who has argued with a spouse who says, "Don't give me that look," knows that our body language can convey volumes about our inner thoughts, sometimes to our detriment. In conversations with those in trauma, we have the challenge of overcoming the tension inherent in such interactions. We must keep our body language loose and calm despite the sometimes-difficult things we are hearing.

To show the speaker that you are engaged and listening, maintain an open posture, facing the speaker head-on. Don't look down at your desk, out the door or window, or at the speaker's hands. Look at the speaker's eyes. Then, throughout the conversation, check in with yourself—are you tense? Are your shoulders hunched? Fists clenched? Mentally scan your body, head to toes. With a deep breath, release any areas that you're holding tension. Without dropping eye contact, do a few body scans throughout the speaker's story.

As the speaker's tension rises due to the recounting of the traumatic event, you may start to feel that tension as well. That flood of tension into our own bodies may cause us to subconsciously adopt a defensive stance—crossed legs or arms, turning away from the speaker slightly, clenching jaw or furrowing brow.

It is not a bad thing that you feel tension in this moment. It is a natural physical response to the story you are hearing—it's your empathy at work. The problem is the defensive stance, because that communicates to the speaker that you don't want to hear this story and the speaker will respond to that, even unconsciously, by slowing down, minimizing, or stopping speaking altogether. So the goal is to keep the tension from causing you to turn away, drum your fingers on the desk, or scowl.

This is why you are doing the body scans. Notice that tension happening and consciously release it. Relax your shoulders and unclench your fists. Slow down your breathing. As long as you are maintaining eye contact and nodding sometimes, you should be able to do this without interrupting the speaker's story or communicating that you don't want to hear it.

The tension that is finding its way into your shoulders, hands, or face, of course, still needs somewhere to go. This isn't an insurmountable problem; you just need to be deliberate about how you release it. The goal is to avoid interrupting the speaker. You want the tension release to be invisible. Slow breathing helps—in through the nose, and out through the mouth. It also helps to find some muscle that you can flex invisibly. Calves are good. Feet and toes. Maybe your stomach, if you can do so without changing your facial expression. Practice sometime on your own, to see if you can flex a part of the body without showing it. Then you'll be ready in the moment when you need it. Be intentional: deliberately flex and release the muscle a few times, specifically to release the tension that the traumatic story is engendering. Once you've mastered this, you will be able to keep your body from communicating a message that you don't want it to—that this story is too painful for you to hear.

Of course, doing these little physical exercises and focusing on your own breathing means you are pulling yourself mentally out of the speaker's story. Isn't that the opposite of what we've been trying to do? We want to stay present, right? Focused on the speaker and the story that's being told? Yes and no. The tension that we feel has to be handled, or else we end up communicating to the speaker to stop talking. What I would suggest is that you do the body scan in a part of the conversation that is slightly less intense. For instance, if the speaker is describing a sexual assault, stay present during the initial details of the assault. Then, when that intense recounting has moved on to descriptions of discussions with the police, for instance, take a slow breath and do a body scan. You can still listen with part of your brain while you're doing so, and it will help maintain your energy and focus through the rest of the conversation.

THIS MAY ALL seem overwhelming at first. Thinking through these concepts ahead of time, however, will help a lot once you're in a situation that calls for them. Spend some time practicing these techniques over the next few weeks. Notice when you are mirroring someone and play around with it by changing your own stance to see if those with whom you are speaking change theirs as well. Notice your body's posture when you are stressed or when you are relaxed. Notice others' body language, as well, and think through what it communicates to you. Try out different question formats and notice how some questions open up the conversation while others shut it down. Try out looping back to someone the words they've said to you: "Horrible traffic! It's so frustrating," "He didn't even call you back," "Now you have to handle twice as much as before." Seek clarification on a story someone is telling by using the speaker's exact language: "When you say, 'He just left out of there,' you mean he walked out the door?" The more you try out these concepts ahead of time, the better prepared you'll be when confronted with someone in trauma, and the better you'll be able to keep your cool—and help the person in trauma.

Finally, if at any point it seems that you are having trouble managing your emotional response, or the speaker is, take a break. "I am so glad you told me this. Thank you. It's a lot to process, and I need a minute. Can we take a quick break?" "Thanks a lot for sharing all that. You've certainly been handling a lot. How can I help you right now? Do you want to take a break? Can I get you a drink of water?" It is better to walk away for a moment, or even for a day, than to force the conversation to continue when emotions are running too high.

# Controlling Your Response

We've discussed empathy and the way we experience the emotions of the individuals telling a story. Sometimes, though, it isn't just that you are experiencing some of their pain. Sometimes what they are telling you is infuriating. They are wrong! That isn't what happened! You feel a wave of righteous indignation—a tidal wave of it—and it's surging through you, and it must come out to correct this horrific miscarriage of justice that is assailing you.

My friend, put a lid on that tidal wave.

I know it's hard.

How can they say these terrible things? Don't they know that isn't true? They must be misinterpreting the situation. I'll just correct them and then they'll feel better.

They won't, though. In fact, they'll feel worse. And, bizarrely, so will you. If you get into an argument over the facts of the situation, you won't convince them of the truth of your version of the story, and instead you'll turn the heat up on an already difficult conversation. There may be yelling. Or crying.

Tell yourself this, over and over again if necessary: you will never convince them.

The reason you won't is because this is really not about their desire to learn the facts. This part of the conversation is solely about telling their story. Until they get that story out, they can't hear what you say. It's like there is a glass wall between you, and everything you say bounces back at you, harder. The only way that wall is coming down is if the person feels heard and understood.

Even if they are wrong, wrong, wrong.

Your job is to sit and listen. To remain present, even if you want to be anywhere else. One trick I like is to pretend that I am a reporter, and later I'll need to write an article explaining this person's story and perspective. *How fascinating*, I think, as they spin out stories of how terribly I treated them. *What an interesting perspective you have.* I focus on my breathing. I keep my expression neutral. I do my best to release the tension in an invisible way. I know that later there will come a time when I am able to share my perspective, but unless the speaker gets out her story, we will spin endlessly around fact and opinion.

If you can muster it, validating the person will speed things up even faster. Meghan Riordan Jarvis, a therapist who often works with those in trauma, says that when people are upset, challenging their views will simply ramp up their frustration. Instead, she validates the emotions behind what they're saying, even if their words themselves are not accurate. Riordan Jarvis says, "Situations loaded with emotion can make us inaccurate reporters of events. In a session, my client might say, 'I can't believe you said my father was a jerk.' I know I didn't say that, but I can still validate the emotion. 'Wow, I can see how frustrating it would be to hear someone call your father a jerk.' I'm not lying by agreeing that I said something I didn't say, but I'm getting at the emotion underlying the statement."[1] This diffuses the tension. Then, once the person is calm, Riordan Jarvis can correct the statement. "I know you felt I called your father a jerk. The point I was actually trying to make was . . ." Because his emotions have been validated, the person can hear that statement and is calmer and more able to focus on next steps.

Let the person talk. I promise it's the quickest way through.

It's also possible, of course, that the person is actually correct. When someone tells us that we or our organization did something wrong, our knee-jerk reaction is often defensiveness. If we can control that long enough to hear what the person is saying, we may learn something important and useful. The key is not just to allow the person to talk, but actually to listen and seek to understand. If the person is incorrect, speak up to control the misperception, but first analyze whether what the person is saying may be true, in whole or in part.

What if what you are feeling is not anger, but disgust? Annoyance? Resentment? Nothing at all? Perhaps the person is telling you a horrible story and you can't generate even the slightest feeling of sympathy. Know that this is also incredibly common and normal. Sometimes, all our brains want is to get away from this uncomfortable conversation. That can show up as annoyance. *Ugh, this is taking forever. Why does he keep going on and on? I really need to get out of here.* Or disgust: *She completely brought this on herself. What an idiot. I'm not going to waste my time listening to all this.*

Alternatively, you could experience a system shutdown. Your brain just goes blank. You see the person talking, and you are watching him, but you can barely process what he's saying; the best you can do is to nod sometimes. Your fingers may grow cold, and your breath become shallower. Time seems suspended.

Again, these are all normal responses. We don't choose how our bodies respond. The key is to see what's happening and take steps to counterbalance it. A deep breath or two always helps. Then try to bring yourself back to the moment. Engaging one of your five senses helps ground you in the present moment and focus on the person in front of you and what is being said. Reach out and touch something—the wood of the desk in front of you, the steel of the chair next to you, your own legs. Notice the pattern on the wallpaper behind the person talking and count out five flowers or stripes. Take a drink of water and think about whether it is cold or warm. Think through the scent of the room you're in.

There may come a time when you are not able to get a grip on your own response. Perhaps you are hearing about something particularly upsetting, or one that brings to mind a hard experience of your own. You do not have to be a robot. Feelings are normal. It's when we try to ignore or hide them that we create problems.

Instead, acknowledge them. Notice that you are having a hard time staying present for the person because you are having an emotional response. Acknowledge this explicitly and ask for what you need. "John, this is really tough. I want to hear what you're saying, but I need to take just a minute for myself so that I can keep being a good listener for you. Do you mind if we have a quick break?" "Hang on a second. Let me process that before you go on; it's a lot."

It's always okay to walk away for a moment. I like to take a walk outside whenever possible. Looking at the sky always calms me down. Even if you can't physically walk away, closing your eyes and taking a few breaths can do wonders. If you need to, it's also okay to adjourn the discussion and come back later. It's much better to call a halt and come back fresh than to force yourself through a conversation when you are not in the proper frame of mind to be helpful.

Finally, none of the above is intended to indicate that you should sit silently while someone abuses you. If the person has begun to attack you personally, shout, or threaten, stay calm and set a firm boundary with safe eyes. Don't interrupt, and take a second's pause before you speak, or else the conversation will ramp up further. "John, you can't call me names." "You're yelling right now. That's got to stop if we're going to continue talking." Repeat the same words, as needed, calmly and firmly, always taking a quick pause before you begin speaking. If that is not working, halt the conversation. "We're going to stop here. I want this conversation to be productive, and we need to take a break so that it can be."

# What if the Person Is Lying?

A challenge may arise where you think that the person is exaggerating, delusional, or outright lying.

They might be. The honest truth is that when someone tells you something—perhaps, "I'm upset because my bike was stolen"—you have no idea if she is telling the truth. Maybe it wasn't stolen; instead, she misplaced it. Maybe she didn't care that much about the bike but is raising the theft with you for some ulterior motive. Maybe the bike wasn't actually hers. She could be wrong on the facts, blowing the incident out of proportion, or fabricating it entirely.

What may surprise you is this: the best way to handle that situation is exactly the same way you'd handle a situation where you believe the person entirely. In fact, your assessment of the veracity and reliability of the speaker is not relevant to this interaction.

In many interactions, the truth of what the speaker is saying will never be relevant. If I am sitting next to a man on the bus and he opens up that he's recently lost his life savings in a scam, I will listen, acknowledge how awful that is, share what I know about scams, point him to resources like where to report scams and how to access financial support, and leave things on a solid ground before we part ways. It doesn't matter if he's lying about the whole thing, simply to get attention. If someone is willing to go to those lengths merely for a listening ear, well, I'm glad I gave him one. It took little from me and perhaps helped someone in need.

In some instances, though, you may need to determine the truth of what the speaker is saying. Perhaps you are a human resources officer who must recommend actions to be taken in response to a complaint. You may be called upon at some point to decide who is telling the truth and who is not. Still, in this first interaction when a person comes to you with a story, the best course of action is to maintain an open and neutral demeanor, without making judgments on truth one way or the other.

Here's why. Imagine that you do not believe the person who claims that her bike has been stolen. You've never seen her with a bicycle, and in fact, she's often complained to you about her bad knees. You have a really hard time believing she currently owns a bike, or even that she ever did.

Your disbelief will show up in a note of suspicion that will be nearly impossible to mask during the conversation. It will become quickly evident in the way you phrase questions, your body language, and the things that you don't ask or say. The speaker will not fail to miss it.

There are a few ways this may impact the speaker. She may grow defensive: "Who are you to question whether that was my bike?" She may begin to doubt herself: "Am I crazy? Did I actually park it where I thought I did?" She may simply give up: "He clearly doesn't believe me. I'll just drop it." In each of those situations, the conversation gets more muddied and confused, the person trusts you less, you are less helpful, and you are less likely to get to the truth.

Law enforcement officers must determine the truth in complex situations very quickly. Their jobs—and sometimes their lives—depend upon it. Here's what they know: "*Unless there are particularly strong reasons to suspect the credibility of the [eyewitness's] story, it should be treated as a truthful statement. If the [eyewitness] is not innocent, but is truly involved in the crime,* that will be uncovered eventually during the investigation and there will be ample time to re-interview her."[1]

The way to uncover the truth is not through suspicion, cajoling, or setting traps. The fastest way to get to the truth is to be open to it. Listen without judgment. Your goal in this moment is not fact-checking. Our memories are affected by trauma in complex ways.[2] Some memories are incredibly precise and unwavering, while others become vague and difficult to pin down. Timelines can get mixed up. When you push too hard on the facts, you can further confuse the person and muddle the story. If you are an investigator who will need to write a report on what happened, first allow the story to come out in the way that the person in trauma wants to tell it. Later, after this conversation, you can come back to get clarification. Give the person room to open up to you. The truth will come out more quickly and completely that way.

There is one caveat to this: don't lead the person to believe that you take everything they say as gospel truth and will be their advocate when you are actually a fact finder. If your role is to determine the truth of what happened so that further action can be taken, it is essential that you remain open-minded until you have heard all of the information. Be honest and clear about your role. "I am an investigator hired by the school to determine what happened. I want to hear everything you have to tell me about this. I am also going to talk to others about it, and gather information from other sources, like police reports and text messages. The question I have to answer here is whether a student violated the honor code. What you tell me is part of trying to figure that out."

If you allow people to think that you believe without reservation everything they say and will push for their version of the facts, it tarnishes the investigation and can breach their trust if later you must walk back a statement of unmitigated support for their version of events. This doesn't change how you listen, just how you speak. You still listen with an open mind, but make sure that the person sharing information with you understands your role.

# When Not to Listen

There is one circumstance where the best course of action is to shut down the conversation. If you realize at some point that the story the person is disclosing is one that needs to be handled by someone else (the security officer, your supervisor, even the police), it is best to halt the conversation unless there is a professional reason you need to continue it (for example, you have a separate obligation to record the event, even if the security officer needs to hear it, as well).

There are two reasons to stop the conversation. First, telling a story of trauma can be difficult, and you don't want to force people to tell you if they are later going to have to tell someone else the same thing. Second, your hearing of the story may vary in small ways from another person's, which can muddy up the record. It is often best, and cleanest, to get the person to the right authority as quickly as possible, for one clear recounting of the event rather than one cobbled together between what was told to you and what was later told to someone else.

Thus, if at some point you determine that what the person experienced is beyond your authority to handle ("above your pay grade," as the feds say), then stop the conversation. "Julia, listen, I can tell that this is something that Lindsay is going to have to address. I don't want you to have to go through it all twice, so why don't I walk you over to her now?" "I'm going to stop you here. What you're telling me really needs to be handled by the police. I'm happy to help you make that call, or support you in any other way I can, but I don't think it makes sense for you to go through all this with me when they really should be the ones handling it."

# Taking Notes

I t is occasionally necessary to take notes while the person is talking. Notes can help with keeping track of what is said and will help you later in the conversation when it comes time to acknowledge what you've heard. Notes are also a record of what is being said to you, which in some cases is necessary, and they may be of assistance if you later must write a report of the interaction.

There are thus a lot of advantages to having notes, but the actual taking of the notes can be a hindrance to connection. Note-taking will make some speakers nervous. They may modify what they say to create a certain impression, or say less than they want, which will not help you in learning the facts or them in getting out what they need to say. Often, it is best to find unobtrusive ways to take notes. Let's consider each of the options for recording notes, in turn. For each of these, it is important that the person knows you are taking notes. When it is optional, ask if the person minds if you take notes. When it is not optional (you'll later need to write up a report or your notes are a required part of a file), explain that you'll be taking notes and why, so that there is no question about the purpose of your recording.

## Typed Notes

For some people, typing is the fastest way to record and makes it easiest to incorporate the notes later into a report. An added advantage is that you won't have to worry later about deciphering your own handwriting.

There are downsides, though. The computer can act as a literal barrier between you and the speaker. The sound of the clicking of keystrokes constantly reminds the speaker that statements are being recorded, which can be stifling. It is difficult to maintain eye contact while you are typing. If you have pop-up calendar or email notices, they can distract you from the speaker. I also find a tendency to slip into transcription when taking notes on the computer, which causes me to miss nuances of meaning that I would otherwise glean through direct observation of body language, pitch, and volume. Even if I do notice those things, I am less likely to note them while typing, instead sticking to a bare recitation of the statement made.

In certain circumstances, all of this might be fine. I tend to take notes on the computer when I am discussing something complex but not emotional. If the report being made to you, for instance, has to do with a complicated financial transaction, and the person discussing it is doing so not to unburden herself but rather to give you an understanding of the facts, taking notes on a computer would be fine. I also take notes on a computer more often when I am talking on the phone, because then maintaining eye contact and avoiding the physical barrier of the computer screen are not relevant. I always let the speaker know that I am doing so, because I don't want him to think that I am surfing the web or responding to emails, and if the person has become emotional or the topic has turned sensitive, I stop typing.

## Handwritten Notes

Taking notes by hand can shore up some of the downsides of typing your notes. The notepad, flat on the desk in front of you, is a less obtrusive barrier between you and the speaker. With a good pen, the writing should be nearly silent. If you develop the skill to write legibly without looking at the paper, you can maintain good eye contact and a strong connection with the speaker. I find that I am more likely to record observations about the speaker and the story with handwritten notes. I will draw arrows or circle topics to which I want to return, which can be helpful later when it is time to acknowledge, share information, and equip with resources.

Of course, this comfort level with handwritten observations could be detrimental in some cases. It is important to remember that notes are sometimes discoverable in litigation. A good rule of thumb is to record only things that wouldn't embarrass you if they appeared on the front page of the newspaper. Another potential downside of handwritten notes is that the speaker may be able to read them. Again, it is essential to be mindful of what you are writing to avoid embarrassment or insult.

## Recordings

Finally, you could record the meeting, either through audio or video. In most circumstances, this will obviously not be possible or desired. If someone drops into your office, you are unlikely to tell the person to hold on while you set up the video camera. If someone is making a formal complaint, however, you may choose to record. A video recording is the best preservation of the meeting, allowing you and others to observe later the demeanor, inflection, and exact wording of the speaker. Recording, whether video or audio alone, also gives you the opportunity to rely on the device rather than having to take notes during the meeting. You may wish to take notes anyway, to assist you later with the wording you choose to reflect back and the information and resources you share, and use the recording as a check on your notes and recollection.

In all instances, you should ensure that the speaker knows and consents to such recording. This is required by law in many states, and in all cases is essential to building and maintaining trust.

As a final note, I would advise that you write a few notes after the meeting. This will give you a moment to reflect on what was said, which may result in additional resources that you could share, and will help you later when you return to check in on the person. It is also a good way for you to close the conversation neatly in your own mind, so that you can go back to work.

# Hearing What Isn't Said

R eady for a real ninja move? Once you've mastered hearing what the person is saying, controlling your own response, and displaying open-minded interest, you're ready to move on to a more challenging maneuver: hearing what the person is *not* saying.

Sometimes the speaker approaches you about a particular topic or episode, but there is some clue in what's being said that shows you that a different issue is in fact weighing on the person. This clue gives you the opportunity to head off a problem before it becomes a bigger one.

Perhaps you work in human resources and an employee, Gina, comes to you to inquire about job opportunities that might be arising soon in the workplace. Gina has worked for the company for more than ten years, and recently got a new supervisor, Mark. Gina is Black, and Mark is not.

As Gina discusses what kinds of positions she is looking for, she keeps saying she hopes for "a better fit." It surprises you a little because Gina has always seemed to thrive in her team. A few times she mentions that Mark might find her "a bit too much." "I do like to express myself," she says with a smile at one point. She also says that she'd like "to be trusted with bigger assignments."

Don't interrupt Gina to ask about it, just note the phrases that keep arising. This phraseology is something you can return to later, after you've acknowledged Gina's stated reason for coming to you. As she's talking, think through whether there might be something more going on. Black women are often penalized for expressing their views or standing out in any way.[1] Is Mark limiting her role and silencing her in meetings? Is he perhaps biased against her?

You may be thinking, "Now I have to worry about what they're *not* saying? Isn't it enough to deal with what's actually being said?" Or even, "I'm not going into all that deep-seated psychological stuff. If they're not being up front with something, it's not my job to go into it."

Here's the thing, though. If someone comes to you about one issue but there is a deeper issue underlying it, that deeper issue will continue to haunt you if you don't address it. You can help Gina find a new spot in the company and perhaps that will give her exactly what she needs in the moment. If the real problem, though, is that Mark is squashing the opportunities of people of color on his team, you can bet that the issue will arise again.

If you do suspect there is an unspoken issue driving the conversation, addressing that can be tricky. If you just say, "Is Mark discriminating against you?" Gina will likely demur. You also run the risk of communicating to the speaker that you weren't listening—she's looking for job opportunities and suddenly you're asking about race? And, of course, you could be wrong.

The open-ended question is your friend here. The question needs to be truly open ended, with no presupposition as to the answer, and presented as guilelessly as possible. "How are things going with Mark?" "Any other concerns?"

The notes you've been taking are also going to be really helpful. Use the speaker's exact words and mirror them back. "You've mentioned a few times that you feel like you might be 'a bit too much' for Mark. What do you mean by that? Can you give me some examples?" If she does, you can follow up with, "How is he with others on the team? Have you seen similar interactions with others?"

Your goal is to signal to Gina that it is okay to go into whatever the underlying issue is. You can't force her to disclose it, but you can let her know that you are open to hearing it and give her some room to discuss it.

Of course, you may be thinking, "The absolute last thing I want is to hear about some racial bias claim. If she's willing just to move to a new position, that is fine with me." Remember, though, that the ostrich approach doesn't work for long. You don't want to learn about this first in a lawsuit. The goal is a healthy workplace, not a quiet morning.

If Gina doesn't take the invitation, though, let it go. You can't force her to discuss something that she isn't ready to discuss. She may come back, and she may not. You have shown her that you are willing to hear what she has to say, and that can make all the difference in the world.

14

# Self-Harm and Harm of Others

Before we go on, I want to say a brief word about some special circumstances. You may at some point be in a situation where you fear someone is a danger to himself or another. Thinking through this situation ahead of time can help you to be prepared if the situation arises.

## Self-Harm

If someone discloses to you that he or she is contemplating suicide, it can be frightening. This has happened to me a handful of times in my life, and each time, the fear I felt left me shaking for days. Many years later, I can still recount the details of each. It can feel like a tremendous responsibility, as if this person's life is in your hands.

Suicidal thoughts are more common than you might think. According to the National Survey on Drug Use and Health, approximately 4 percent of adults had thoughts about suicide in 2017. That represents 10.7 million people. Approximately 1.4 million actually attempted suicide.[1] The number who succeed is far lower than that. I hope that you notice the discrepancy between those figures—almost 90 percent of those who think about suicide never actually attempt it.

Suicidal thoughts are most often the product of depression or another mental health disorder that requires professional treatment. People may be reluctant to seek treatment because of the stigma around mental health challenges and suicide. If you can get comfortable talking about mental health and suicide, you can fight stereotypes against seeking treatment and recovery, helping the person to get the assistance they need to get better.

Of course, when someone says something that makes you wonder if the person has been having suicidal thoughts, you don't know how serious the threat is. So ask. Display an open and neutral curiosity. Contrary to common fears, asking if people have suicidal thoughts does not put the idea in their head, or put them at more risk.[2] Instead, it simply makes them feel less alone.

Therefore, if someone says, "God, sometimes I just want to end it all," follow up. It might be a joke or an exaggeration, or it might be a tentative call for help. Sometimes, people say things like that to see if you'll panic. If you do, they can backpedal and say, "No, just kidding, of course I'm fine." Remain calm, and just ask the question: "Is that something you think about?" Try to keep your face neutral—again, you're a reporter, trying to learn the facts. It's a yes or no question. If the answer is a genuine no, then fine, let it go with an easy, "You know I'm always here if you need me. I care about you." If it's a yes, give yourself a pause to take a breath and collect yourself if you need it. Then thank the person for telling you. The person trusted you with something really scary and that likely induces feelings of vulnerability. You now have the ability to help, which is such a gift.

Then keep asking questions. Try to ascertain how serious the situation is, how long the person has thought about it, and how specific and lethal the plans are. "Is this something you've thought about before? How often?" "When did this all start?" "Have you thought about how you'd do it?" "What have you thought about doing?" "Do you have a gun [or pills or whatever method has been mentioned]?"

The responses to these questions can give you a sense of how much danger the person is in. A person who says, "I don't know, maybe I'd jump off a bridge or something," is likely in a different place than someone who says, "I have a loaded gun in my bedside table. Every night I take it out and stare at it. I don't know when I'm finally just going to do it."[3]

It is also helpful to understand some of the risk factors for suicide. If you see some of these, it may be worthwhile to inquire about suicide even when the person doesn't mention it first. These risk factors include:

- Recent significant loss or threatened loss (that can be related to money, work, a relationship, a school failure, family rejection, or something else)
- Depression or other mental health disorder including, importantly, addiction
- Preparations for suicide (giving away possessions, putting affairs in order, talking about a time when "it will all be taken care of")
- Hopelessness, guilt, self-hate, or perceived burdensomeness
- Withdrawing from family and friends
- Taking risks that could lead to death, like reckless driving
- Extreme mood swings
- Changing eating or sleeping habits[4]

It can be frightening to ask, but again, try to keep an open and calm demeanor. "You're definitely going through a lot lately. How are you holding up? Are you struggling? Ever think about hurting yourself?" "You seem really down. I'm worried about you. Please know that I care about you and want to help. If you're ever thinking about hurting yourself, you can talk to me. Is that something you've considered?"

Let the person know you care, and that you are concerned. "I'm so sorry you're dealing with all that." "That must be so scary." "That sounds awful." Avoid minimizing or glossing over the risk by saying "I'm sure it'll pass," for instance. You don't know that it will. Instead, let the person know that suicidal thoughts can be overcome with the help of a professional.

The goal of this conversation is to get a sense of the level of danger the person is in and then get the person to seek professional help. There are incredible resources out there for people who are suicidal. The National Suicide Prevention Lifeline is 1-800-273-TALK (1-800-273-8255) (Spanish: 1-888-628-9454).[5] The Crisis Text Line can also be accessed any time of day or night by texting 741741. You can call or text these services yourself or encourage the person to do so. Your workplace may have access to counseling services at low or no cost, through the Employee Assistance Program (EAP) or otherwise.[6]

Try to persuade the person to access these services. "Wow, you're carrying a lot. Must be exhausting. How can we get you some help? Do you have a counselor?" "I hate that you're shouldering all this alone. Do you know about the suicide hotline?" "I'm amazed at all you've been handling. It's too much, though. We've got to get you some help. How about if I give EAP a call? They're right here, they're free, and they're confidential." "You deserve help from people who are smarter about this stuff than me. Let's find you some real counseling." If the person accepts the resource, ask if it would be all right if you follow up with the person, or with the resource, later on.

If you determine that the person is in immediate danger—has the means to access a lethal method of self-harm and is determined to use it—then you will need to take affirmative protective action. Call your office security team or 911. You may be concerned about overreacting and taking yourself away as a trusted support for the person, but for such people you are also making clear that you value them and that they need help. Getting them the services they need may be exactly what is necessary to get them onto the road to recovery.

Frighteningly, the number of suicides at work is on the rise.[7] If your workplace has been affected by suicide, I am so sorry. That is a devastating experience for all whose lives were touched. A wide array of emotions is normal in response, including guilt, anger, bewilderment, depression, and fear. There are resources out there to help. The National Action Alliance for Suicide Prevention has a *Manager's Guide to Suicide Postvention in the Workplace: 10 Action Steps for Dealing with the Aftermath of Suicide*.[8] The guide includes advice for immediate, short-term, and long-term steps to take, as well as sample internal office notification letters and public statements.

# Harm of Another

What if, instead, the speaker discusses harming someone else? Perhaps a woman says that her ex-husband is driving her so crazy that sometimes she wants to drive by his house and shoot out his windows. Again, an open curiosity will help here. "Do you think about that?" Or: "Do you mean that seriously?" "Have you ever done anything like that before?" If it's clear from the response that she was exaggerating and is not a threat to anyone, then you may feel all right letting it go. Most of the time, when people say things like that, they are letting off steam. When confronted with someone who takes them seriously, they are a little horrified and bend over backward to show that they don't mean it. If nothing else, you are showing them that language threatening others is not something that you will let slide, and they will be more careful with their language around you.

What if the speaker doesn't back down? What if, instead, she doubles down? "It wouldn't be anything he doesn't deserve." "You know what? I have driven by that house every night for a week and every time I see that woman's car. It would be so easy to hurl a brick in there and knock that ugly smile off his face."

While I'm sure you feel anything but grateful for this information, it truly is a good thing that you're hearing this. A person who is speaking in earnest about harming another, with specific plans to do so, is a danger. You now have the opportunity to intervene and perhaps to interrupt a violent event.

First, let the speaker know that you take what's being said seriously. "That sounds terrible. I'm worried that you're going to hurt him." "That would be a crime."

If the speaker doesn't back down and you have concerns that he or she will act on the threat, it is wise to end the conversation. "I can't go along with what you're saying. I think we need to end this here." "This really bothers me. You're talking about violence and that's not okay." It's possible that this will jog the person into laughing off the matter ("Oh, come on, I wouldn't really do anything"), and perhaps it truly was an idle threat. It is still important to end the conversation here, for two reasons. First, it makes clear that idle threats are taken seriously and will not be tolerated in your presence. Second, it gets you out of the presence of a person who may be violent.

Afterward, make notes of the encounter and discuss it with your supervisor and security team. Make sure to bring up any concerns for your own safety as a result of the interaction, so that you can make a protection plan. If you are sufficiently concerned that there is a real threat to the safety of another person, call the police. Dial 911 for emergency assistance, or 311 for nonemergency police response.

Finally, you should know whether there is some affirmative reporting obligation that you have when it comes to harm of another. Every state has a law that covers mandatory reporting of child abuse and neglect. Most states require reports only for certain professionals (for example, law enforcement, day-care workers, and pediatricians), but eighteen states require all citizens to report child abuse and neglect.[9] Many states also have mandatory reporting laws that cover abuse of elders or other vulnerable adults.[10] Even if you aren't a mandated reporter, though, if you have some information that leads you to believe someone is in danger, you should report that to someone who can help.[11] Reports can be anonymous.

# Winding Down

Usually, people's stories will wind down naturally. They will finish sharing what they want to share and will be ready to shift to you for the next phase of the interaction. But some people have trouble reaching that point. They may keep talking and talking, and it becomes clear that the discussion is no longer productive. They're repeating themselves, and not sharing any new information. Or perhaps they're getting increasingly emotional. You may be employing all of the right techniques—eye contact, mirroring, seeking clarification, and looping—but instead of calming down, they're growing increasingly agitated. It's as if they have gotten stuck in a spiral and need a hand to get out of it. Alternatively, maybe they have gotten off on a tangent, and the discussion is no longer covering the topics they came to you to discuss (though remember the caution in Chapter Thirteen about hearing what isn't being said, for a possible reason for those diversions).

If you are the listener, you are the one who is under less stress, and thus you need to be the one who maintains the temperature of the conversation. If you allow yourself to get frustrated with the speaker, or to mirror the speaker's stress response, the conversation will veer off and become unproductive. Have you heard the expression "Be a thermostat, not a thermometer"? A thermometer rises or lowers with the temperature of the room. A thermostat sets the temperature. Be intentional in setting a cooler temperature. The best way to do this is to remain calm yourself. Take deep, slow breaths. Find some nonintrusive way to release some of the tension you're feeling. Use mirroring to your advantage in a proactive way, by consciously adopting an open stance—lean back in your chair, force your shoulders down, notice if you are furrowing your brow and release it. Slow down your speech. Allow moments of silence. These few techniques alone may be enough to cause the speaker to peter out. If not, you'll have to be more assertive. You'll have to interrupt.

This is much more effective if you've been quiet for a while. Wait for a slower moment in the tirade and say, quietly but firmly, "Okay." Or, "Yes." "I hear that." "Got it." Repeat this a few times if necessary. Often, this will surprise people enough that they will stop talking. Sometimes it's as if they've forgotten you're there.

If not, you'll have to be stronger still. Say the person's name, firmly but calmly. You may repeat the name, but don't yell, under any circumstances. You're counterbalancing the stress, and thus you have to be especially calm.

If that's still not working, you'll have to be firmer still. "Joe, I hear what you're saying." You can lean forward at this point, if necessary. A pointed look helps, too, or a hand up in a "Stop" gesture. Again, you are not yelling, and you have to employ calming techniques on yourself before you do any of this. You don't want the speaker to feel attacked, because that will lead to defensiveness and further emotion.

Remember that all of these techniques are much more effective if you've been in a more relaxed stance for a while. It's the change in your demeanor that will command attention and pull the speaker from the spiral.

Once you have the speaker's attention, maintain control of the conversation. It's time to shift to the next stage, Acknowledgment.

# STEP TWO

## ACKNOWLEDGE

People don't care how much you know
until they know how much you care.
—THEODORE ROOSEVELT

# Introduction

Listening is an essential first step in supporting someone in trauma, but the response we give is also important. If we minimize the person's experience or imply that she is at fault, we can exacerbate the negative implications of her experience. In contrast, an acknowledgment of what has been shared demonstrates respect and gratitude to the speaker for sharing something difficult. This section covers the types of responses that are helpful and those that are not, as well as issues that can warp the words we say, like victim blaming and distancing assumptions.

HANNAH WAS AN English teacher at a remote and picturesque private high school on the East Coast. It was a job she'd longed for, and that she loved. Young and energetic, she thrilled in her work with students—seeing their eyes open to the hidden images in the texts they read, refereeing their vigorous arguments, and delighting in their barbs over parts of the books that seemed implausible.

Eric, another teacher in her department, had welcomed her warmly to the school. Light conversation and an occasional lunch over her first few months helped her get settled in her new job. Eventually, though, Hannah grew uncomfortable with their relationship. Eric had confided that he was getting a divorce. Hannah sympathized as best she could; she'd never been married. He seemed to be coming to her office more and more frequently, though, and leaning on her more than she'd like. She began trying to avoid him, by eating her lunch off grounds and taking work home rather than doing it in her office.

Eric, though, would not be put off that easily. He kept stopping by her office and making comments that went from complimentary to cringe-inducing. Eventually, she decided she needed to be more forthright with him: "Eric, it's clear that we want different things. I think it would be better if we stopped spending any time alone together. If you have a work matter to discuss, please raise it, but I would rather that we not discuss personal matters anymore."

Instead of making things better, though, the conversation seemed to send Eric into a tailspin. He began texting her repeatedly, asking if she would reconsider her stance and go with him to dinner, a movie, a cup of coffee. Hannah decided the best course was to ignore him, fearful that any response she gave only seemed to add fuel to the fire. Then the messages turned darker.

"I can't stop thinking about you."

"You were radiant in today's assembly. Nothing makes me happier than seeing you smile."

"I drove by your house last night. I like to imagine you in there, sleeping peacefully. What do you wear at night, I wonder?"

Hannah's office was two doors down from Eric's, and she found herself feeling nauseated every day as she went into work. She began avoiding her office whenever possible and keeping her door closed when she had to be there. She considered changing her phone number, maybe even moving. Finally, Hannah decided she could not let Eric's inappropriate behavior continue to affect her work and her sense of safety. He was in the wrong, not her. She went to her department chair, Robert.

Robert listened thoughtfully as Hannah explained the history of the texts and interactions with Eric, and her own responses. He nodded sympathetically as she discussed her anxiety about seeing Eric at work, and her fear that he might show up at her house in the middle of the night. Hannah, who had worked hard always to be seen as professional and competent, felt humiliated that she had to discuss such personal matters with her department chair, but she began to relax at Robert's kind face and open demeanor as she unfurled her story.

Then he spoke.

With a gentle half-smile, he said, "What you need to realize is that Eric's been going through a really hard time. You know, he got divorced not too long ago. I'm sure it's been difficult for him to be alone after what? Fifteen years? You're a bright and engaging young woman, and I can see why his head was turned. But I've known Eric a lot longer than you, and let me tell you, he wouldn't hurt a fly. He'll get it together. Just give him some time. In the meantime, take the compliment! Must be nice to be so desirable. Oh, and one more thing. I'd appreciate it if you didn't gossip about this. He's in a tough spot, and I'd hate to see his reputation suffer for this little bit of flirtation."

Hannah flushed as her stomach dropped. Was she overreacting? A "little bit of flirtation"? Eric had said some really creepy things! Was Robert telling her it was her fault for being "bright and engaging"? She wasn't gossiping! Hannah was furious with herself for sharing all this embarrassing information when it was clear it wasn't going to help anything at all. She mumbled something incoherent and hurried out of Robert's office.

Robert figured he'd sorted the situation out. Hannah, though, was left feeling unheard, powerless, and with nowhere to turn.[1]

# Why We Acknowledge

H ow you respond to people who have disclosed a traumatic event to you can have long-term ramifications for their healing from the event. Negative reactions can silence them, so that they never share the experience again, and can affect their physical and emotional health.[1] Blaming responses lead to lower self-esteem and less outreach for other supportive measures, while positive responses are associated with increased coping strategies and a decrease in self-blame.[2]

Even more interesting, recent studies indicate that the person to whom the story is told can make a difference. When someone in a position of authority is told the story and responds to it in a supportive way, the person in trauma is more likely to access support than if the person told a friend or family member.[3] Anne DePrince, professor of psychology at the University of Denver and an expert in interpersonal trauma, says, "If someone in a formal capacity responds to a survivor in a way that is helpful and responsive, that opens the door to accessing all sorts of resources."[4]

Institutional responses that are *not* supportive, however, can likewise have a stronger effect. When people in trauma go to an institution that they are a part of for support, and the institution responds in a negative or unhelpful way, that institutional betrayal can be a separate trauma that creates a new and separate harm, which can itself create anxiety and exacerbate trauma.[5]

Listening is essential, but so is an appropriate response to what they've said.

Even where our responses are less tone-deaf than Robert's, many people bobble the reply to a disclosure of a difficult event. When we hear something painful, we may have an impulse to rush past it to move onto ground where we feel more comfortable. There are a few ways this often appears.

- We launch into our own story. Imagine the scenario above, but with Hannah telling a friend instead of Robert. The friend then says, "God, that reminds me of Andrew. Do you remember him? What a jerk. It took me years to get away from that guy! I thought I would have to quit." And so on.
- We try to talk the person out of the problem by saying the person is misinterpreting the situation or blowing it out of proportion. "Are you sure that's what he meant? That doesn't sound like him." Or, "I'm sure it was a joke." "You probably misheard him." This is often intended as kindness—if I show you that you are wrong about what's upsetting you, you will no longer be upset. As anyone who has received such responses is aware, though, they are at best unhelpful and at worst gaslighting.
- We leap to problem solving or giving resources. This is another response borne out of an effort to help. "Well, you need to tell him to knock that off!" "Tell his supervisor right away." "Send him an email, so you have documentation." "Here's the number of my therapist. He's fantastic. He'll sort you out."
- We change the subject. When we hear something truly awful, it is difficult to process it and often we simply want to keep it from entering our brains altogether. Sometimes, you see this happening

in breathtaking ways. "Mom, I have to tell you something. Jay assaulted me last weekend." "It's been raining *all day*. I don't think it's ever going to stop. It's a good thing I got those bulbs planted when I did." It can happen more subtly, as well, though. "I've got to be gone next week. My brother has brain cancer, and I'm flying out to be with him for his surgery." "We can push the staff meeting to the following week, I guess. When are you back?"

Many of these responses are intended to be caring and thoughtful. They seek to help or to empathize with her. Some of them will be perfectly appropriate—later. It is good to share resources with people in need. That therapist might be just the right person to help. Maybe your story of overcoming a similar experience is incredibly on point and illuminating. It's possible that they did misinterpret what was said. Here's the problem, though. If they don't feel that you heard them, they won't be able to hear you.

I'm going to say it again, because this is so important and such a hard concept to get: if the speakers don't feel that you *heard* them, they will not be able to hear what you are *telling* them. Missing this small, essential part of the conversation is where a lot of difficult conversations go off the rails. You'll feel like you've solved the problem, so then why is she still upset? Or, you told him he was wrong about what happened; he should feel better now. But he definitely does not. First, you have to show the person that you heard what was said. You have to acknowledge the story.

Before we can go on with the conversation—sharing resources, correcting perceptions, or anything else—we have to acknowledge that this person has just shared with us something painful, becoming vulnerable, trusting us with a hurt, and seeking our help. The acknowledgment may, and in fact should, be brief. It can take just a minute. That one minute, though, can be incredibly important in shaping what comes later, both for you and for the speaker and her healing.

# Silence

The first thing to do when someone has shared a story of trauma with you is nothing at all. For a short moment, just be still.

The person has wound down and finished his story. It may be a horrible story. You may want to immediately say how sorry you are or to begin sharing about the person you know, the book you've read, or what helped you in a similar situation.

Don't. Not yet.

All of those things may eventually be helpful, but first, sit. For just a breath. Give the buzzing in the room a chance to settle. Look the person in the eye and take a breath. Allow the story to settle.

It doesn't need to be a long moment, and indeed, if you let it stretch too long, it may make the speaker uncomfortable. *Did she understand what I said? Is she mad?* It's just a short moment, but that brief pause does two things. First, it gives the speaker a moment to shift gears from sharing an uncomfortable story to being ready to listen. Second, it gives you a moment to collect your thoughts and check in with yourself. How are you feeling? Sad? Disgusted? Angry?

Acknowledging your own feelings allows you to get a handle on them. Fists clenched under the desk? Jaw tight? If you know that you are feeling angry, you can accept that and take a second to acknowledge it. *I'm feeling really angry that he's having to go through all this. I'm furious on his behalf.* Simply acknowledging it can help you bring those feelings under control, so that you can then move to a place of being present for the other person, instead of the anger seeping out in strange ways.

Anger is not the only response that can warp a conversation. Maybe you're scared. *I don't know what this is going to do to Jocelyn. I have to tell her. She's under so much stress as it is.* Or anxious—whether about what the person has told you or something else entirely. *Oh my god, we've already been talking for twenty minutes! I have to get this email sent by five o'clock!*

My own common and incredibly unhelpful response to an uncomfortable situation is that I often smile or laugh. As an example, I briefly worked as a waitress at a restaurant in Georgetown, a busy shopping area in Washington, DC. One day, four women came in loaded down with bags of purchases and each ordered a tall fruity cocktail. I carefully balanced my tray of drinks from the bar, down the stairs, and across the restaurant—where I promptly dumped it all over one of the customers and her bag of new clothes. Did I apologize, jump to clean up the mess, offer to make amends? Nope. I laughed. It wasn't that I thought it was funny, it was that I was nervous. Let me tell you, it did not make the situation better. (I wasn't fired on the spot, but I quickly recognized that was not the right job for me and left on my own within a week.)

Of course, inappropriate smiles or laughter can lead to more damaging results. One heart surgeon smiled broadly as he broke the news to a wife and children that their father had died on the table.[1] That inappropriate smile was devastating to the family. When the widow subsequently filed a malpractice suit against him, she admitted that she did not know about the level of medical care provided in the surgery but said that the suit was brought due to the doctor's "chilling, horrifying smile."[2]

Just a moment of silence, one breath, can allow you to check in with yourself, figure out how you feel, and get your emotions under control.

Recognize your own anger, nervousness, fear, tension, or whatever else comes up. This allows you to stay present for the speaker and respond appropriately. It also allows you to be sincere in how you respond. It's okay to acknowledge your own feelings: "That sounds awful." "That just sickens me." "This makes me angry." "It's really hard to hear that." "I don't know what to say."

The key is that it should be quick. If you get too caught up in your own feelings, for instance by your own fears the story has brought up, you shift the focus onto yourself when it should be on the person who came to you. Try not to cry or to let your anger bubble over. It's a quick acknowledgment, and then move on. You don't want the person who came to you for support to feel that you're the one who needs support instead. We've likely all had friends or colleagues who turn every story into an opportunity to recount their own anecdote. Or, as one woman noted, a particularly tone-deaf response from a friend she told about her cancer diagnosis was, "You have to get better! What would *I* do without you?"

It's okay to have emotion, of course. Sometimes, it's really difficult not to. The horrible things that some people have to endure can take our breath away. Take an extra second to get your own response under control if you need it. Acknowledge it to the speaker: "Sorry. That was tough to hear. I just need a minute." But then, rein in your feelings. You can come back to them later, on your own. This moment is the one you have with the speaker, who has recounted to you something very personal and vulnerable. Keep your focus on the speaker and on responses that are helpful.

# Thank the Person

After you've taken a breath and allowed the room to settle a bit, it's your turn to talk. So what do you say? The first thing to say, perhaps counterintuitively, is "thank you."

It is incredibly difficult to share a hard story. If that person is sharing her story with you, she is entrusting you with it, and with her own vulnerability in opening up about something painful. For some people, it may be a story that they've never shared with anyone. Even for those who have shared the story before, it can be painful to retell it.

I teach a class at American University on victim rights. One semester, for our last class of the term, I asked a colleague to join us. She had worked in victim services for decades and had spoken all over the country, to audiences of thousands. She had been a journalist and thus was a professional storyteller. She was also a survivor. I asked her if she would share her story with the class, to make real what we'd studied about victimology and the criminal justice system, and also to show the students that those who've endured unspeakable horrors can go on to do amazing things. She accomplished both of those aims, in spades. She was compelling, articulate, clear, polished. Her voice never quavered. Afterward, as the class left, she grew quiet, and her shoulders sank. I approached her as she sat alone by the front of the classroom, so diminished from the bright and strong energy I normally saw from her.

"It's always hard," she said to me.

I understood. Even for someone who has told his or her story a dozen times, a hundred times, telling that story of pain can still be difficult. It still means reliving the experience, pulling up the pain, the visceral details that are, it turns out, quite easy to recall, despite the intervening time. It takes effort to share that story. This truly is a gift to you. They have honored you by sharing their experience, giving you a glimpse into who they are and what they've gone through. So thank them.

We also do this because for the person who has just shared a personal story, that moment before you begin to speak is a moment of incredible vulnerability. He doesn't know if you are going to laugh at him, blow off his concerns, gossip about him to others, or otherwise use his vulnerability against him. Because of this, he is likely steeling himself for what may be a painful blow. Preparing those defenses distracts him. He isn't fully open to hearing what you say in that moment, because part of him is readying for battle. By thanking him, you show that you will treat him and his story with respect. You aren't going to attack him. His defenses will drop just a little; you may even see a visible release of tension—an exhaling of breath, shoulders dropping, hands unclenched. Now that he has calmed down some, he will be better able to hear what comes next from you.

Thus, the "thank you" serves both to honor the person who shared with you something difficult, and it helps prepare him for the next step in the conversation. In terms of the actual words, it doesn't need to be anything profound or awkward. It is a simple acknowledgment. "Thanks for sharing all that." "I had no idea. Thank you for telling me." "Thanks for coming to me with this." "That sounds awful. Thank you for trusting me with it." "I know that wasn't easy to say. Thanks for saying it."

# What Not to Say

After you take a breath and say thank you, it'll be time to say something more. This isn't strictly necessary, but most people will want to say more to acknowledge what the person has shared. In terms of what to say, a conversation can't be overly scripted or else it feels stilted and unnatural. It is often like a dance between two people. It's okay to let your instincts guide you and to respond to the person in front of you in a way that feels sincere and intuitive to you.

There are, however, a few statements that almost universally feel lousy to someone in trauma and yet that get said all the time. You are well on your way to a positive interaction just by avoiding these comments.

## "I know how you feel."

Kenneth Feinberg, who administered the September 11th Victim Compensation Fund that awarded payments to those who were injured or lost loved ones in the September 11 terrorist attacks, learned this lesson in a stark way.

> I remember one eighty-three-year-old man came to see me after 9/11. He said, "I lost my son. Mr. Feinberg, a father should never bury a son. I'll never be the same. Doesn't matter how much money you give me."
>
> I made the mistake of saying to this very nice man, "This is terrible, I know how you feel."
>
> He looked at me. Nice man. Tears. "Mr. Feinberg, don't ever tell people like me that you know how I feel. You have no idea how I feel. You have a tough job, but those words ring hollow. They're pretentious, they're robotic."
>
> Well, I'll never do that again.[1]

At that point, Feinberg had likely met with hundreds of people who had lost loved ones on 9/11. He knew a lot about what they were going through. But he hadn't yet met this man, who was grieving this son.

The problem with "I know how you feel" is that it presumes that all grief is the same, when in fact each situation—and each response—is unique. You may have lost a loved one. But your own grief over losing your mother (or even over losing your own son) is not the same as someone else's grief over losing his son.

This statement also shuts down conversation by saying, in effect, "You don't have to tell me; I already know." Allow the speaker to explain to you his or her feelings. Even if you've heard it before, the person needs to express it.

## "Everything happens for a reason."

This statement is akin to others that can irk those going through a difficult event—"God wouldn't give you more than you can handle," and "It was her time." Both presume that a higher power has decided on a large-scale course of action, and that the trauma that has befallen the speaker is merely one piece of that larger plan, the reason for which will one day be revealed.

For those who are not in trauma, I think this can give a lot of comfort. For the person in acute trauma, however, it can ring hollow. As one survivor tweeted, "When people tell me it was all part of God's plan so that He could eventually use me to expose evil in the church, I always scream inside. What kind of god predestines a kid to be repeatedly raped by a minister so that 30 [years] later, she can expose evil? That IS evil."[2] It also has a smack of pretentiousness about it: "You, in your grief, cannot see the larger plan, but it is quite clear to me, over here in my comfort and wealth." Further, it presumes a belief in a higher power, which many do not have. Statements like this can distance you from the speaker when you want to make connections.

## "It will all work out for the best."

The problem, of course, is that sometimes it will not. Sometimes, those who are sick do not get better. Those who have lost their life savings may never return to their previous standard of living. Even where the person recovers, a difficult experience leaves emotional scars.

## "You need to put this behind you."

The person will eventually begin to heal, but only if he is able to experience the loss. There is no set timeline for this. The best thing we can do as listeners is to support the person where he is and allow him to go through the process that he needs to go through. Similarly, telling him that, "Your children need you to be strong," or "Your mother wouldn't want you to be grieving like this," distorts the grieving process by adding guilt to it.

## "I have a grief story too."

You probably do. Your grief story may be incredibly similar, and it may be a positive, inspiring one, about how you were able to overcome a difficult circumstance. This is not the time for it, though. In this moment, your only job is to hear what this speaker is saying. If you launch into your own story, you are taking the focus away from her and onto yourself. It may be appropriate to share your story at some point, but not in the moment after someone has just shared her story with you.

What about a brief "I've gone through something similar myself"? This may seem tempting; it is an easy way to build connection and trust. If the speaker knows that you have a similar experience, she will find it easier to relax and believe that you understand, without having to go through all of the details.

There can be downsides to this, though. First, it can still pull the focus to you—the person may want details, and it can be hard to shut that down without creating the impression that the speaker was wrong for sharing a painful story with you. Second, it can create shortcuts in the conversation when there shouldn't be.

To understand why, imagine that someone tells you that he recently bought a house. You bought a house once, too, and you tell him so. "Ah, so you understand," he says, with a rueful smile. You bought your house, though, ten years ago. Today, the market is much hotter. The speaker went through a year of open houses, frantic late-night bids, lost properties, and finally an accepted offer well over the asking price. The connection he feels with you is false; you don't actually understand what he went through. Because he believes you do, though, he cuts off further explanation. You don't realize what you've missed, nor does he realize that you have no true sense of his experience. When we are talking about the sale of a house, this may be fine. If we are talking about a traumatic event, though, this kind of foreclosing of conversation can be really detrimental.

Finally, it also can create the impression that you will be his ally. You've gone through this; you are on his team. When you are in a professional environment where someone may look to you to advocate for him, this can be a dangerous assumption. What you've gone through is never exactly what the speaker went through, and while you may feel quite sympathetic and want to help, it is unfair to create an expectation that you fully understand and can advocate on his behalf.

# "I could never endure everything you've been through."

When my oldest child was two years old, I had twins. Thus, for a while, I had three children under three years old. When I would take them for walks, holding the hand of the two-year-old and pushing the twin stroller with my other hand, I would get a constant barrage of acknowledgments from well-meaning passersby: "You've sure got your hands full!" and "I don't know how you do it!" and "You're a better woman than me!" I knew that these people were trying to be nice, but still, these statements irritated me. What I heard was, "Better you than me!"

For me, this was actually a happy occasion, to have young children in the house. Imagine, instead, that the person to whom it is said has lost both parents in the space of a month, or has a disability and a husband who just lost his job. Statements like these are intended as a compliment—"You are stronger than me." Instead, though, they tend to come off as, "Whew, thank God I'm not in your shoes." The speaker didn't choose the situation, either, but he can't get away from it; he has to endure. As would you, if it happened to you. Instead of building rapport with the speaker, these statements distance you from him.

# "At least he went quickly."

Or, at least there was time for everyone to say goodbye. At least he never knew it was happening. At least she's not suffering anymore. At least you weren't injured. One woman was telling a friend about the yearlong litigation she was engaged in with her condo board. Her friend's response: "At least you don't have kids yet."

All of these "look on the bright side" statements tend to minimize what the speaker is currently experiencing. Not only should you not be sad, you should be grateful. It could have been worse. But right now, the speaker isn't feeling grateful. The speaker is feeling sad or angry or frustrated about what did happen, and that is okay to feel. These statements cut off the discussion of the pain this person is experiencing. This moment is not about moving on or getting away from the pain. It's about sitting with this person in her feelings, right now.

## "God never gives you more than you can handle."

The idea that a higher power is doling out tragedies in a fair manner is so appealing. The fact is, though, that sometimes life isn't fair. Sometimes, people get more than they can handle. Sometimes, as a friend says, you get dealt a tough hand.

This statement can create the impression that they are supposed to be strong enough to withstand it, and if they're not, there is something wrong with them, or they are letting God down. It often makes the speaker feel weak, instead of strong. It can discourage people from getting help. In addition, if the speaker doesn't believe in God, or is, understandably, feeling really angry with God in that moment, this may upset her or create distance between you and her.

**PLEASE KNOW THAT** if you have said these things in the past, or if you say them in the future, you haven't failed the person in need. The statements aren't ruinous, and if said with kind intent, that sentiment will come through. They aren't the most helpful things to say, though. What all of these statements have in common is that they tend to ease our own discomfort, while not serving the person who is in distress. We lean on them because we aren't sure what to say; we are uncomfortable and want to fill the silence. For many of them, we are trying to convince ourselves that the pain the speaker has can be contained and will not last. Unfortunately, that may not be the case for the immediate future. These statements also tend to shut down the speaker instead of allowing room to express grief. This moment won't last forever; the speaker will, of course, go on. But allow the speaker this moment to feel messy, scary emotions without minimizing or rushing past them. It truly is the most effective way to help.

# What to Say Instead

There are many things that may be helpful to say. This section discusses some of them. These aren't blocks that can be fit into any situation; they are simply ideas to get you thinking. Your acknowledgment in a particular conversation should be sincere and based upon those with whom you are speaking and what they've shared with you.

## "I'm so sorry."

This is probably your instinct to say, but often people skip over it or feel that it sounds trite or overly expected and that they should say something more profound. It's the standby for a reason, though. Note that this is not an apology that takes responsibility. It's an apology for what they're going through. You could even say, "I'm so sorry to hear that," or "I'm sorry you've been dealing with all this." Research shows that apologies that don't take responsibility nonetheless can build trust and empathy by demonstrating kindness and care.[1] We'll discuss apologies that take responsibility in Chapter Thirty-Three.

## "It's always okay to talk to me."

For someone who is clearly anxious about having shared something, this can be incredibly relieving. It lets the person know that coming to you wasn't a mistake and that you will continue to be a resource.

## "You're doing a great job."

In my experience, people in trauma usually think they are handling it poorly. A person going through a difficult time may be having trouble with even the basic functions of life. Getting up and readying to go in the morning, managing the commute, fulfilling job requirements, sometimes even eating and sleeping, can seem insurmountable. This can make people feel inept, and their own negative self-talk exacerbates the pain they're feeling and creates a vicious cycle. You can help with this by acknowledging that what they're going through is difficult and praising them for handling it well.

## "It's okay to take care of yourself."

Similarly, reminding the person to give herself space to heal can be helpful. When we are struggling with something difficult, we have to treat our response to it like a part-time job. Rest, proper eating, talking to a friend or journaling, and exercise can all help us to get through the challenging time. Remember not to make people feel guilty for the things they haven't been able to do, so avoid statements like, "You have to make sure you're eating properly." The key is to give permission, not an admonishment.

## "That sounds awful."

Or scary or tough or horrifying or whatever it legitimately sounds like to you. This is a brief, human connection, acknowledging the person has shared with you a story of a painful event. I often pair this with an apology: "I'm so sorry. That sounds devastating."

## "What you're feeling is normal."

For those in pain, there can be a lot of guilt that they are not handling it as well as they're supposed to. They aren't supposed to laugh and have fun or, alternatively, they shouldn't be so sad all the time. They shouldn't be short-tempered or so exhausted they can barely get out of bed. All of those are normal reactions, of course. It's normal for the same person to cycle through each of those emotions, and more, in the course of a week or even a single day. The judging of the feelings, though, adds an unnecessary layer of guilt on top of the primary feeling, which clouds the feeling and makes it take longer to get through. It can be an incredible relief for people to receive permission to feel exactly what they're feeling.

## "I can see how hard this is on you."

This acknowledges that they are going through something difficult, and it gives them permission to admit to the pain that they have likely been trying to keep a grip on.

THE GOAL OF all of these statements is to create room for the speaker's feelings and convey that you are understanding and not judging. There are plenty of other things that are good and caring and helpful to say. This list is not exhaustive; it is simply intended to give you ideas and a general sense of what kinds of things are more helpful than others.

# Avoid Judgment

efore we move on, it is important to consider an issue that can warp the words we say, and the way we say them, so that even if we say all the right things, they will nonetheless wound the person we are trying to help.

## Why We Blame Victims

Most people have heard the phrase "victim blaming" and understand intellectually that this is a bad thing to do. And yet, most people do, at least to some extent, blame victims for what has befallen them. When we hear about something horrible that happened to someone, our minds instantly go to "What time was it?" "Where were you?" "Were you by yourself?" "Did you leave your door unlocked?"

Psychologists say that we do this because of what they call the "just world bias." We tend to believe that people get what they deserve. To test this, scientists showed study participants videos of two men solving puzzles and told them that afterward one was randomly assigned to receive a larger cash reward. Participants rated the one who received more money as smarter, better at solving puzzles, and more productive—even though they knew that the reward was arbitrary.[1] Similarly, when study participants were shown videos of a woman who was asked questions and received (fake) electric shocks for wrong answers, they criticized her and said she deserved it. Interestingly, they were less likely to criticize her if they had the chance to help her. When the study was changed so that participants had the option either to give her a reward for a right answer or to take away the shocks for a wrong answer, all chose to take away the shocks—and all judged her more highly than those who had no ability to stop the shocks.[2]

We want to believe that life is fair and that what goes around, comes around. If we have the power to make it so, we do; if we don't, we engage in mental gymnastics to convince ourselves that the bad that befalls people is at least a little bit their fault. We do this because we want the world to feel safe, ordered, and sensible. We want to believe that we can protect ourselves and our loved ones, that we aren't at the mercy of random acts of horror. Thus: If something bad happened to you, what did you do to make that happen? Because if I know, I can avoid that thing, and I will be safe from what happened to you. And so, when a nonsmoking marathoner gets lung cancer, we ask if he lived next to a factory. When a biker gets hit by a car, we ask if she was wearing reflective gear. When someone is assaulted, we ask if she was drinking. We search for the mistake people made that led to the pain they are suffering.

Of course, the world is not nearly as fair as we would hope. Horrible things happen to very good people all the time. Life, in short, is not fair, despite our best efforts to make it so.

## The Effect of Victim Blaming

The belief that those who have had bad things befall them brought it on themselves is not merely inaccurate, though. It is also incredibly damaging. When we search for the action of the victims that led to the pain that befell them, we communicate that they are not as deserving of our sympathy as they would be if they were free of blame. This affects their ability to cope with the incident and to heal from it. Survivors of sexual assault who received a blaming response to their disclosure of what had happened to them later suffered worse self-esteem and lower coping skills than those who did not.[3]

What is particularly insidious about blaming victims is that it mirrors some of the same conversations that the victims are likely having with themselves. Victims want to believe in a just world, too, of course. For them, the desire to blame is perhaps even more keen: if they can point to the action they took that led to their suffering, they can be very careful to avoid that action in the future and therefore keep themselves safe from experiencing the same negative experience again. What if I'd called the doctor on Friday? I should have left earlier; only drunks are on the road after midnight. An experienced prosecutor I know has tried dozens of fraud cases, seen hundreds of schemes, and helped thousands of victims. Yet when she herself was defrauded, she thought, "Of course it's my own fault for falling for that. What an idiot." One sexual assault survivor blamed herself for three decades after a rapist attacked her in an alley with a knife when she was thirteen years old. She felt it was her fault because she'd been wearing boxer shorts, and the elastic waistband made them easier to pull down. If she'd been wearing more fitted clothing that was harder to get off, she reasoned, maybe he wouldn't have attacked her.[4]

The speaker is having those thoughts for the same reasons that you are—if I didn't in fact have any control over the situation, I am always vulnerable to being victimized. If, instead, something I did caused it, then by avoiding the things I did to cause it, I can make myself invulnerable. Your statements to the victim that underscore his secret fears about his own blameworthiness will sting and hold a long impact, precisely because they mimic what he is already telling himself—if only he had made different choices, he would have been safe. Of course, it is not truer when the victim says it to himself than when you say it to the victim. Both are based on the fallacy of control. The victim did not have control of the situation. The victim was acted upon and did his best to protect himself.

To be clear, no matter how a person was dressed, how trusting, how foolish, or how drunk, no one ever deserves to be hurt. When people take advantage of others to harm them, they are at fault, not those they took advantage of.

Fine, fine, you say, but what if those statements are true? What if the person did in fact make some dumb mistakes that put him at risk? What if he is partially to blame?

That all may be right. In fact, most interactions that lead to trauma are complex, with many threads to untangle. It's perhaps true that if he hadn't walked down that alley he would not have been mugged that night. Have you ever walked through an unsafe area? Think through some of your own near misses, which could easily have gone the other way. If they had, would others say that the injury that befell you was at least partly your fault? We all need to take the steps we can to protect ourselves, *and* we don't deserve to be taken advantage of. If people violate us, it is their fault, not ours.

## Blame and Post-Incident Behavior

Actions that people take after a traumatic event can be even more confounding. It is often difficult to understand why people who have been victimized respond the way that they do. People stay in abusive relationships when all they have to do is walk out the door. They disclose that they were sexually assaulted years afterward and then can tell you specific details about the incident, but not when or where it happened. Sometimes, these behaviors make us question whether the person is telling the truth about the nature of what happened, or whether something happened at all.

The Harvey Weinstein trial in New York provided a stark example of this. A key issue in the trial was that the two accusers had maintained relationships with Weinstein after the alleged rapes. As the defense counsel said, "You don't tell him you love him in 2016 and you are tired of being a booty call in 2017 and call him a predator in 2020."[5]

Those who work with sexual assault survivors know that it is common for survivors to maintain relationships with their rapists after the assault. This is partly due to that same just world bias. None of us like to see ourselves as a victim, being acted upon by forces beyond our control. Our minds will do somersaults to convince ourselves that we are in fact in control. We tell ourselves that we had more power than we did and that perhaps we had even gone along with it. "If they can now conceptualize this as a relationship, they can feel they have control, whereas before they didn't feel they had control," said psychology professor Elizabeth Jeglic. "Sometimes it can take years for someone to realize it was rape."[6] In fact, in a study by the US National Library of Medicine, more than 60 percent of rape survivors did not acknowledge what had happened to them was rape, instead calling it "bad sex" or "miscommunication."[7]

Further, as amply seen in the Weinstein incidents, there may be outside pressures to maintain the relationship, and to do that you have to convince yourself that the person is not an abuser. As psychiatry professors Joan Cook and Jessi Gold note, "When the abuser is seen as an authority figure, with an omnipresent powerful presence who controls their livelihood and financial prosperity, some women feel they have no choice but to be compliant. At the very least, they know they will interact with their abuser again post-assault, and so they adopt an adaptive indifference to cope. They may convince themselves he won't do it again, or they may turn the blame inward, wondering what they did to deserve their abuse."[8] "Many of us have experiences with difficult bosses, and we put up with them because we don't think we have a choice, because we need the job," adds psychologist Lisa A. Fontes, an expert in sexual assault and intimate partner violence.[9]

Even outside of the work context, there can be incredible pressure not to disrupt a peer group by accusing someone of assault, as many college students know well. The National Institute of Justice found that 85 to 90 percent of sexual assaults reported by women in college were perpetrated by someone they knew—and fewer than 5 percent were reported at all.[10]

Thus, there are many reasons that those who have been harmed may not react in ways that seem logical. Fortunately, it's not up to us to decide in that moment whether to believe them or judge their actions during or after the incident. You don't have to make any decisions right now about what happened, when it happened, and who did what that ultimately led to the trauma. In fact, as discussed in Chapter Ten, attempting to do so will instead impair your ability to get the full story, if that is your aim. Beyond that, these questions of guilt and responsibility will cloud your ability to be present for the speaker in that moment. Instead, listen without any judgment. It's not your job to pass judgment; it's your job to hear this person's story. Later, there may be additional information that calls into question this person's responsibility. For now, though, just hear what the person says.

# Distancing Assumptions

Another issue that can impair the interaction is to assume things about the speaker that are not true. When people tell you a personal story, it is natural to feel close to them and thus to want to highlight similarities between you, by saying to them things that would comfort you. It is important to be careful, though, in doing this, that you don't assume things about the speaker's background that may not be true. When you do this, you can inadvertently create distance when you are trying to build connection.

Imagine a coworker you don't know well tells you that she's recently been diagnosed with cancer. You feel awful and are eager to show that you care. You notice that she's wearing a wedding ring and ask, "How is your husband coping with all this?" You are undoubtedly trying to show an understanding that her trauma can impact those who love her, as well. If she is a lesbian, though, what you are communicating to her is that you don't know her at all and may even disdain her for her sexual orientation, since you assumed that she was straight. Instead of feeling closer to you, she feels distant and a little fearful.

If you say, "I'll keep you in my prayers," your intent is to show that you care for the person and will ask God to help them. For someone who is not religious, though, that can sound patronizing and sanctimonious. On the flip side, if you say to someone who is devout, "I'll keep you in my thoughts," that can come off as smugly politically correct and pointless—prayer does something; thoughts do not.

If you say, "For me, the best therapy is a good long run," you create distance from those who are not able-bodied or as physically fit as you. It can also feel denigrating for those for whom mental health is a much bigger issue than can be solved by a good long run.

We make assumptions all the time. We assume that the person in front of us has a particular socioeconomic background, has loving and supportive parents, and that their race and gender can be easily identified. Sometimes, we are wrong about all of these things, and more. We can't avoid all errors, but if we try to be mindful, we can make fewer of them.

Some may say, "Oh, good grief. Now we have to police everything we say? Most people are straight. What's wrong with assuming that someone wearing a wedding ring is married to someone of the opposite sex?"

In truth, it's not a horrible assumption. You'd be right most of the time, and it would have exactly the impact that you want—the person would feel closer to you and understood. But sometimes, you would be wrong. The other person, who came to you for support, would leave feeling misunderstood. You would have a dissonant, difficult interaction with someone without knowing why. Even those who are straight may feel uncomfortable, recognizing the assumption you made without basis.

Some forethought and care can avoid this. Think through what assumptions you are making and if your assumptions could be wrong. It helps to listen and mirror the language the person is using. Did she say "husband" or "spouse"? Use the same term she did. Open questions are also good. "Do you have some support around you?" "How are you taking care of yourself?" We take care to avoid assumptions not because we think people are too fragile to correct us but because, through these assumptions, we inadvertently create distance between ourselves and the person with whom we are speaking, when that is the last thing we want to do.

# Resist the Urge to Fix It

Perhaps you are a fixer. You are highly competent. You know a lot about a lot of different topics. You have a broad community of friends who are experts in various fields. You have read extensively and have a library full of books on important subjects. Most of all, you want to help. When you see someone in pain, it causes you emotional pain, sometimes even physical pain, to watch them suffer without intervening.

This is a wonderful impulse. It is a testament to your kindness and the generosity of your spirit. It will also not serve you well in this moment.

Wouldn't it be so wonderful if we could fix it? If someone came to us with a devastating personal problem and we could hand them a book and their sadness would vanish in a puff of smoke? I wish it were so. I would buy a thousand copies of that book and hand it out to every person I met.

There is no such book, of course. For better or worse, what people in pain need from you is not a book, or a referral, or medical or legal advice, or words of wisdom. What they need is for you to sit with them in their pain. You help them simply by allowing them the space to experience their messy emotions.

This can be a relief. You aren't required to have the magic solution. You don't have to be wise or knowledgeable. You merely have to be brave enough to share this space with them, knowing that there is no solution or easy way out. It feels so inadequate, and yet it is the only—and the best—thing we can do.

There will come a time for you to share what you know. Once the person has been acknowledged and feels heard, they will be more able to hear you. Then it is time for the next step in LASER, when you share information.

# STEP THREE

## SHARE

No matter how difficult and painful it may be,
nothing sounds as good to the soul as the truth.
— MARTHA BECK

# Introduction

For some interactions, the first two steps of LASER are all that is needed. If a friend or family member has experienced a trauma, listening and acknowledging are the two best things you can do. If you do those (again and again if necessary), you will have fulfilled your role as a supportive friend and loved one. If, instead, you are in a work environment and the person in trauma is coming to you for help, you will need to do a little more. The last three steps of the LASER method are intended for those who are in some position of authority and the harmed individual seeks your help with a problem. Those situations call for the next three steps of LASER: Share. Empower. Return.

Sharing information is a key part of handing back power and dignity to someone who has been injured. Sharing information also builds trust. It shows that we are reliable sources of information and that we in turn trust the traumatized person with that information. It is important when we share information that it be accurate, and thus it is worthwhile to do some investigation prior to sharing facts. Facts are not the only type of information we can share, though. We can also share information on the process—what steps will be taken next and who is responsible for what. We can share information on our values and on the organization's values. Finally, being up front about what we don't know or cannot share is also, in a way, sharing information. It demonstrates that we are not hiding something and that more is being done to collect information. It is helpful to pair this with a discussion of when information can be shared.

This section covers the types of information that can be shared as well as how to share information in a way that a person in trauma can understand it. It also includes a discussion of apologies—another key way to restore power and dignity.

**BY THE TIME** Leilani Schweitzer got to California, she was exhausted. Her son, Gabriel, suffered from hydrocephalus, or excess fluid in the brain, caused by a stroke in utero. At four months old, he'd had a shunt placed in his brain to drain the fluid. For a time, it worked. Gabriel grew into a strong toddler with rosy cheeks and soft chestnut hair. A smile for everyone he met, Gabriel was a born politician who lit up every room.

Then, at twenty months, he suddenly began vomiting excessively, which Leilani knew was a sign of shunt failure. She rushed him to their local hospital in Reno, Nevada. The doctors there diagnosed a stomach flu, held him for a few days, and dismissed him. He wasn't getting better, though. Leilani knew there was something else wrong. She called the pediatrician's office again and again. Finally, she had Gabriel seen by a neurosurgeon, who agreed that Gabriel needed immediate and substantial help. He arranged for Gabriel to see the experts at Stanford Children's Hospital. Leilani packed her sick toddler into the car and headed over the Sierra Mountains, traveling hundreds of miles to Palo Alto.

Leilani arrived spent, but relieved. After the stress, the uncertainty, the endless prodding of Gabriel, she'd made it. He was with the best of the best, and they would know what to do. She sank into the chair at his bedside and lay back, responsibility lifted from her shoulders.

The nurse caring for Gabriel saw the bags under Leilani's eyes and the hollow look within them. She had seen so many tired parents before. It was clear that this poor mother needed to rest, but she was right next to the monitors that blared every time Gabriel shifted. She silenced the alarms so that Leilani could rest. Leilani thanked her and fell into a deep sleep for the first time in days.

Hours later, Leilani was jerked awake as someone shoved her chair aside. The room filled with people, commotion, and the shouted words, "Code Blue!" The stress in the room was both palpable and unmistakable. Leilani knew instantly that her son was gone.

What she learned later is that the nurse, in trying to care for Leilani by silencing the alarms in Gabriel's room, actually turned off the alarms everywhere—including in the nurses' station and on her own pager. Then, when Gabriel's heart stopped, no one knew, and so no one came to revive him.

The manufacturer of the monitoring system later explained that they didn't believe that anyone would go through the trouble of clicking through the seven screens necessary to silence the alerts, and so they did not install a failsafe. They were, tragically, wrong.

When a medical error happens, the instinct of those responsible is usually to circle the wagons. Lawsuits are costly. The average payout for a medical malpractice claim is nearly half a million dollars,[1] which doesn't include legal costs. If the wronged person doesn't know the facts, though, it is a lot harder to sue.

Avoiding lawsuits is not the only reason people don't share information, though. Imagine how it would feel to know that your mistake led to the death of someone. Now, imagine looking that person's loved one in the eye. Excruciating, right? You would do anything to avoid it. Hiding serves multiple purposes. The easiest, and presumed safest, path is to avoid, cover up, and move on as quickly as possible: deny and defend.

That's not what Stanford did here. First, Stanford conducted a thorough investigation to determine what happened. It uncovered the nurse's effort to help, her misstep, and the system failure that allowed it to happen. It then met with Leilani and explained to her exactly how and why her son had died.

For Leilani, this transparency made all the difference. It gave her the peace of mind that can come only with truth. Sometimes we think that if we don't tell people the facts, we will spare them; that we can protect them from the awful truth of what happened. In reality, though, the opposite is true. If we don't give them the truth, they speculate. They ruminate. The horrors they imagine are more awful than whatever the truth is. In providing the truth, we allow understanding and peace.

That is partly why the Truth and Reconciliation Commission in South Africa sought to flush out the truth about the horrors of apartheid. One woman heard the testimony there of her husband's killer, a man named de Kock. "De Kock is the only one who helped us retrace the steps of what really happened," she said. "You have no idea how much of a relief knowing the truth about my husband was. De Kock brought us the truth so that we can be with our husbands, understand what happened to them, and then release them again.... Now I can mourn properly because this has helped me retrace his steps in life in order to let him go in death."[2]

Thus, in sharing the truth of what had happened to Gabriel, Stanford allowed Leilani the peace that comes with understanding. Leilani isn't the only one who was helped. Due to Stanford's investigation, the manufacturer of the monitoring system issued a warning about the lack of a failsafe to all who had the system, thus ensuring that the error that killed Gabriel would never kill another child again.

Leilani did not sue Stanford. In fact, now she works for Stanford.[3] She is the assistant vice president for communication and resolution at Stanford Health Care, meaning that it is her job to help other families understand what happened when they lose a loved one at the hospital. She helps those like herself get the information they need to heal.

# 26

# Why We Share Information

I saw again and again in my years working with victims that one of the hardest things about being victimized is the loss of power. We want to be in control of our fate. We want to know that our actions determine our outcomes and that the life we will live is the one that we make for ourselves. Unfortunately, this is not always the reality. We get sideswiped heading to the grocery store, swindled by our ministers, and devastated by illnesses. It's not fair. We are acted upon, subject to the whim, negligence, or cruelty of someone else, or of fate itself.

This part of the LASER process is about handing back some of that power. Knowledge, of course, is power. From secrets on the playground to insider trading, those who have information have more power. When injury befalls us and we don't know why, that makes an already-difficult situation worse. It adds an insult to the injury.

Sharing information, in contrast, establishes trust and restores dignity. When we give information to someone, we are telling her that we trust her to act appropriately on that information. We allow her to decide how to use the information. We hand her back some power.

Establishing trust is essential. For individuals who have just shared something difficult with you, your sharing in response demonstrates that you trust them too. If you can show them that you are open and honest with them, you are building a solid foundation for what may be a long-term interaction.

Demonstrating that you are honest and will provide reliable information also means that the person is less likely to turn to outside sources for information. Those outside sources can include anything from gossip, to the press, or even the courts. When people file lawsuits, it's often so that they can obtain information.[1] In many instances, it's not the money that matters; what people really want is to know what happened.

We can't fix everything. Sometimes, it seems that we can't fix most things. But the least we can give someone is the truth.

# Why It's Hard to Share

S haring information is not always easy. There are a few reasons for this.

## We Don't Know

First, it's possible that we legitimately have no information. The person coming to us with a disclosure is the first we've heard of this issue. We certainly don't want to get ahead of ourselves by asserting facts that may not be true. Having to walk back information can breach trust. It's important that we be reliable and trustworthy. When you don't know the facts, it's fine to say, "I hadn't heard about this." You can offer to follow up later when you know more: "Let me see what I can find out, and I'll get back to you." That can be paired with sharing one of the other forms of information—process or values, for instance. Of course, it is essential to follow through on a promise to investigate.

## We Don't Want to Share

Maybe we do know information, but we don't want to share it. Perhaps the information is embarrassing or damaging. It puts us or the people or institutions we care about in a bad light. The temptation to avoid or obfuscate may be great.

Decisions around sharing damaging information should generally be made in conjunction with leadership and counsel, where appropriate, but often, sharing damaging information—quickly, clearly, honestly—is the best course of action. The information will likely come out eventually anyway, and not in the way you would have chosen. In the meantime, those who were hurt have suffered further for not getting the information that would help restore their dignity.

## We Have Privacy Concerns

In contrast, we may have information but not be able to share it. For instance, we may be concerned about another's privacy. Privacy for the speaker in the present conversation must mean privacy for all with whom you deal. It is important to be forthright about this: "I can't share with you the results of those interviews, because I need to ensure for those speakers the same privacy that I want to ensure for you."

## We Are Barred from Sharing Information

There may be other considerations beyond privacy, as well. In the criminal justice system, the assurance of a fair trial means that it is essential not to share information from one witness with another. If a victim is also a witness, it is important not to damage her testimony by, for instance, sharing with her information from another source, like the defendant, the police report, or another witness. In the midst of a civil lawsuit or investigation, as well, there may be barriers on the sharing of information.

It is worthwhile, though, to scrutinize whether there may be reasons to share information even in anticipation of or in the midst of litigation. As discussed in Chapter Thirty-Three, plentiful research in the medical malpractice field shows that sharing information in the short run can yield much more favorable outcomes in the long run. Discuss with your team and with counsel, if necessary, whether it makes more sense to share information sooner.

**THE FOLLOWING CHAPTERS** set forth a few categories of information to share, so that even in a situation in which it seems you have nothing at all to say, there is still a way to provide information. The categories of possible information to share are: facts as currently known; process; values; and what we don't know, but hope to learn. Not all will work for every situation, but in most situations, at least one will.

# Share Facts

f a person has come to you following a difficult event, sharing information with him can be incredibly empowering. The best thing you can share is whatever facts you know about the event.

Thus, if your company has been the victim of a data breach, share what you know about the breach, including when it happened, what you know about the organization that committed the breach, how many were affected, what information was taken, and what steps have been taken thus far to avoid further dissemination of information.

If your school has learned of a bullying incident on the playground, share with the parents of the children involved all of the facts that you have learned about when the incident happened, what led up to and followed the event, and what steps the school took to address the matter.

The information you share should be as specific and far-reaching as possible. As Leilani Schweitzer says, "Transparency is not the view of an event from 30,000 feet above, where shapes are fuzzy and details impossible to see. Transparency is an explanation from the ground, it is look me in the eye and explain until I stop asking questions."[1]

When necessary, it's thus worthwhile to do at least a preliminary investigation before talking with those affected. It can be frustrating if the person to whom you are looking for help has no information at all. It can also make your organization look unprofessional. Thus, find and question those involved who have information on the timeline, the incident, those affected, and any steps taken since. Gather and review any necessary documents. Take notes yourself, so that you understand the full story and know that you can explain it clearly. Highlight any gaps and try to fill them. If you can, have those with knowledge of the facts in the meeting with you, so they can answer any questions you can't.

Of course, you must weigh taking the time to do an investigation against the importance of early intervention. The longer you wait before communicating with those affected, the more their anxiety grows. This is also when rumor and negative thinking flourish. Your goal should be to move swiftly to gather the facts, and share them as completely as you can.

One CEO told me about an incident in which an employee threatened violence against another. "I'm going to get my gun and come down there to find you," the employee said to a coworker after an argument. Fortunately, the company had already installed security protections for their office, but the question arose of what information to share with the employees. Some on his team advised not sharing the information. It would just cause widespread anxiety, they reasoned. Best to keep it quiet. The CEO, to his credit, recognized the flaw in this reasoning. "You think they're not already talking about it?" he responded. "That story is spreading like wildfire." He chose to make an announcement to all those in the office warning that there had been a safety threat, that security measures were in place, and more information would be provided once it was known. The anxiety in the office lessened, and happily, the employee didn't make good on his threat.

Give yourself, or your organization, time to gather information, but don't fail to reach out, even if just to say, we are investigating and will share more when we know more. This can establish an early trust and give you more time to investigate.

# Share Process

What if you don't have any facts to share? You had not heard of this incident before the person came to you, or it's not a subject on which you would have facts. Facts aren't the only thing to share. It's also helpful to share process information: what your role is. What you will do with the information you received. What happens next, and after that. Who else must be consulted. When certain steps will be taken. When and if the person will hear back from you.

For instance, imagine that an employee comes to tell you that he has been in an accident and will need accommodations, as well as physical therapy, over the next six months. You could share how decisions around accommodations are made and who in the office is responsible for those accommodations, as well as how to apply for flexible work options.

All of this may seem obvious to you. Perhaps it is available in a pamphlet or in written form on your internal website. It's still worthwhile to go over it.

For someone in trauma, the sense that there is a process in place can be incredibly soothing. "You aren't the only one who has ever gone through something like this," you're saying. "In fact, we have a whole process in place to handle it. You have done your part; now let us take over for the next steps."

Allowing others to understand the process also invites them to feel a part of it. New Zealand prime minister Jacinda Ardern was widely lauded for her leadership during the coronavirus. In particular, her communication style was credited with garnering trust and inspiring safe behavior in a difficult time. One piece of Ardern's daily briefings was a clear explanation of the process that would be used for determining what would be open and when. The government's four-level alert system was released and explained two days before the full lockdown was announced, and throughout the lockdown Ardern discussed the process used for making decisions about what could be opened.[1] As New Zealand succeeded in its lofty goal of eliminating coronavirus from its shores, a national poll indicated that 92 percent of New Zealanders approved of the strict measures that had been imposed.[2] Because Ardern communicated clearly about her government's decision-making process, citizens understood and were willing to adhere to its directives.

A final point on sharing process information is that it's important to remember that those who have just shared a story of something difficult may not be in the best frame of mind to receive information. In fact, they may not be processing it much at all. That's okay. It's still helpful to go over it. The goal of this part of the conversation is not solely to convey information. It also turns the conversation to a more neutral, easier ground. It shifts toward next steps. The person has come to you with a difficult situation. They have shared their story with you and thus feel vulnerable. You have acknowledged that they shared with you something difficult. Now it's time to shift gears. Sharing process for next steps helps with that.

# Share Values

I t can also be helpful to share your organization's values with respect to the issue at hand, or even your personal values. "We have a zero-tolerance policy on bullying." "Our company's leadership has committed to ensuring a safe, welcoming workplace for all employees." "I take allegations like this very seriously."

Again, it may seem unnecessary—your organization's commitments are on the website, maybe even on the wall. But, like the sharing of process information, it can place people's experience within a larger context and create a sense of relief—there is an institution here that is committed to certain values that are relevant and helpful. They are not alone. There are others who are here to help, and who are committed to fairness, security, and to one another.

As Aaron Lazare discusses in his book *On Apology*, one of the hardest things about feeling wronged is that it causes you to question whether you and the wrongdoer share common values. "How can I ever trust him again? He doesn't even know what he did wrong. I feel like I never really knew him."[1] This sense of a rift in the community can make you feel alone and uncertain. By sharing personal or institutional values that are contrary to the wrong suffered, we demonstrate that the person is not alone in believing that the harms they've suffered are not acceptable.

Reiterating your organization's values, though, can of course be a double-edged sword. If you share them, you will be held to them. If you are in an organization that you cannot say, with a clear conscience, adheres to the values it espouses, it may be better not to recount them.

# Share What You Don't Know
# or Can't Share

W hile it may feel uncomfortable to some, in some circumstances the best thing to say is, "I don't know."

You may not. Someone walked into your office and what she told you is all you know of the situation. It's okay to be honest about that. "This is the first I've heard of this." "I didn't know any of this was going on, so I'm going to need to do some investigation to learn more."

Then you can discuss what you hope to learn—what additional people you may need to talk to, what facts you may need to uncover. "Let me see what I can find out about who wrote that memo and what went into it." "I'll need to talk to Alex, of course." "I'll raise this with the IT folks to see if they can track what happened." "I'm not sure what the process is, but I'll find out."

This helps for two reasons. First, it shows that you are not hiding information. You simply don't know the answer. Second, it shows that you take seriously what she told you and will follow up. Remember to take notes about what you've said you'll do, so you don't fail to follow through. This person has placed her trust in you; it's important not to let her down.

What you want to avoid is guessing. Don't share what you imagine probably happened, or what you heard someone else say but haven't verified. It is essential to build trust in this conversation, and if you show yourself to have inaccurate information, that will cause the person to doubt what you say in the future.

What may feel even harder to say than "I don't know" is "I can't tell you." This is so uncomfortable that many people try to avoid having to give that answer, even to the point of pretending not to hear the question or not responding to emails or phone calls. Again, though, being up front about this will build trust much more than simply evading the question. Simply explain that you are not able to tell all that you know, and why. The person will be able to handle it and in fact will be grateful for your honesty. "I can't share with you what we have learned because as we conduct the investigation, it's important that each person's recollection be able to stand on its own, without being influenced by what someone else says." "As I mentioned, I'm going to keep confidential what you told me. I have to do that for others, as well. That's why I won't be able to tell you what I hear from someone else." "I'm not going to be able to share everything with you as the investigation unfolds, but you can always ask me questions, and I will answer as best I can."

If possible, tell the person when you expect that more information can be shared. "Once the investigation is complete, I'll write up a report. I will share that with you before it's final." "As we learn more, we'll update everyone by email." "We'll have a follow-up meeting to share the results."

# How to Share Information

As you share information on facts, process, values, and investigation, remember that those with whom you are speaking may still be in the throes of a traumatic response. As discussed in Chapter Four, that means that they may have adrenaline flow that impairs their ability to process information or remember facts. It's still worthwhile to share the information, but be thoughtful about how you share it.

- First, speak in short, clear sentences. A winding discussion of your company's values will get lost. Instead, "Student safety is our top priority." "We respect one another here, and that goes for everyone."
- Second, repeat yourself. Have you heard that old tip for presentations, "Tell them what you're going to tell them, then tell them, then tell them what you told them"? That will serve you well here.

Find multiple ways to rephrase the same information, particularly if it is important information that you know they'll need later. "I'll take my notes from this conversation and type them up in a report. The typed report is the first step, and these notes will be the basis for that. After I write up the report, based on these notes, I'll . . ." It may seem ridiculous, but it helps so much. I even do it when I teach—if there is a key takeaway, I say it at least three times. It's not easy to process information orally. Repeating helps.

- Third, for critical information and dates, write it down. You should say it, too, but important information, particularly deadlines, should be written down and handed to the person to take with him. If there is some recurring process in place, it's worthwhile to create a brochure or flyer that explains the process, with key steps highlighted. This is helpful even when the information is available online. Giving the person something tangible helps keeps the information front and center. You can also then go over the written materials with the person, pointing to or circling the deadlines or other key information, to help lodge the information in the person's memory.

These tips should help the individual to understand and retain the information that you provide. It is still likely that he will miss parts of what you've said or will forget it soon afterward. That's fine. You can follow up with an email or check in by phone or in person later to reiterate any important points.

In addition, sharing information is not the only aim of this part of the discussion. You're also shifting gears. The individual may have shared something difficult and you've acknowledged that. Soon, he'll have to go back to work or take some other next steps. He will feel more able to do that if he's had a chance to collect his thoughts and shifted to feeling more capable. I think of it as knitting the person back together. Through your discussion of facts, process, values, and what you don't know, you are changing the tenor of the conversation so that he is more ready to take further action.

# The Role of Apology

At some point in the conversation, it may occur to you that you should consider apologizing. Apologies can be incredibly healing—or they can be frustrating, misleading, and damaging. In *On Apology*, Aaron Lazare explains that we experience offenses against us as an assault on our dignity, or a debasement. Thus, an apology is needed to restore that dignity and raise us back up to an equal footing with the wrongdoer. When someone feels wronged by another and that person's apology does not take responsibility, instead of repairing the relationship, the apology actually worsens it. We have all probably experienced the frustration of feeling wronged and the person who hurt us saying, "I'm sorry your feelings were hurt." Of course, sometimes we know that we aren't responsible. If someone comes to you distressed over statements made by her boss (and that's not you), then "I'm sorry your feelings were hurt" may be entirely appropriate. In that instance, the "I'm sorry" is about expressing sympathy, rather than taking responsibility.

Thus, it is worthwhile to spend a little time thinking through the different types of apologies and analyzing how to deliver a good one. There are apologies that acknowledge a difficult situation without accepting responsibility for it ("I'm so sorry your mother is sick"), apologies that accept personal responsibility ("I am sorry that I did that to you"), and apologies that take responsibility on behalf of a group or organization ("We are sorry that we did that to you").

## Apologies That Do Not Accept Responsibility

If there is no implication that you or the organization you represent is at fault, a quick apology can come across as kind and build trust and rapport.[1] This is simple and straightforward: "I'm so sorry you're going through all this." "I'm sorry to hear that; I had no idea."

As you do this, it's important to remember that you don't actually know all of the facts at this point; you have heard one person's telling. Thus, do not, through your response, lead the speaker to believe that you accept wholeheartedly all that has been recounted. It's possible it is completely true and all investigation will bear that out. It may be, though, that another person has a different version of the story. It is also possible that competing accounts of the same sequence of events may be true to each person's perspective. It is essential that you not judge all that has happened before you have even investigated.

You can be supportive of the person speaking to you in this instance without creating an expectation that you are their advocate and will always side with their version of events in the future. Thus, it's not, "I'm so sorry he did that to you," but rather, "I'm so sorry you've had such a hard time." "I'm sorry you've had so much to handle." You can follow that type of apology with one or more of the other statements set forth in Chapter Twenty-One, as appropriate.

## Personal Apology That Accepts Responsibility

What if, instead, the person believes that you are at fault? He's come to you in anger, feeling wronged, and looking for a response?

First, consider whether you do feel remorse, and if an apology would help. Does what he's saying make sense? If so, again, a quick apology can help. "I'm so sorry. You're right, that was lousy. I won't do it again." "I'm sorry. Sometimes I try to be funny and I miss by a lot. How can I make it right?" In reality, even if you think he was perhaps equally to blame for the botched interaction, or that your own actions were justified, consider whether it's worth the fight. For something minor, a quick apology can smooth ruffled feathers and let everyone get back to work.

If you are unsure what the person's complaint is, it is all right to ask some clarifying questions. The trick is not to be defensive. Some humor or self-deprecation may help. "I'm 100 percent sure I'm a jerk sometimes; I just want to make sure I understand how I was a jerk this time, so I can avoid doing it again in the future." Without the self-deprecation, it would be along the lines of "I'm not sure I'm understanding what you're saying. Is it [restate]?" Then, once you understand, a quick apology. "I'm sorry that I was late and disrupted the meeting." Remember that an apology is not "That's not how I meant it" or "You misunderstood me." Just accept the criticism, apologize, and move on.

It may be, however, that what the person is bringing to you is bigger than a quick apology could rectify. Perhaps your actions have harmed someone grievously. For an apology to be effective, it must do three things.

1. *Accept responsibility.* If an apology contains a "but," as in "I'm sorry, but I was just doing what Mark told me to do," or "I'm sorry, but that wasn't what I meant," it's not an effective apology. An apology has to take responsibility for your own actions, not deflect responsibility to someone else—including the person who is coming to you for an apology. If the person is looking for you to take responsibility and the best you can do is, "I'm sorry you were upset," or "I'm sorry if I offended anyone," that will not further the conversation. The person will leave feeling unheard and dissatisfied. It's better to give yourself a break and time to think through your role and for what you can take responsibility. It may be uncomfortable.

Leilani Schweitzer, who works with medical employees on how to navigate conversations with those injured following an unexpected medical outcome, encourages people to think through their hesitation to accept responsibility. "Are you willing to sit with the truth of what happened, in order to give someone back their dignity?" She has found that when people can explain to someone they've hurt what they did wrong and apologize, they feel freer and able to go back to work. "I've seen doctors on the verge of leaving medicine altogether who were able to continue practicing because they were able to apologize."[2]

A true apology that takes responsibility will be specific about the actions you took that harmed another. "What I said was insensitive and hurtful." "I forgot to run the last system check, and that's why the information didn't go out on time."

2. *Apologize.* Say the words. "I'm so sorry." "I regret what I did."
3. *Make amends.* The person to whom you are apologizing wants to avoid the same thing happening again, either to them or to someone else. Some part of the apology, then, should include a corrective action. This can be anything from "I will be more thoughtful about my language and how it impacts others" to "We have new checks in place now, to make sure what happened to you won't happen again." The amends may need to include both some effort to rectify what happened to the individual, as well steps to avoid future mistakes. In some circumstances, the amends may include an offer of compensation.

# Organizational Apology That Accepts Responsibility

What if the person is angry not with you but with your entire organization? A corporate apology is similar to a personal one—it takes responsibility, expresses regret, and offers recompense. As noted in an article in the *Harvard Business Review*, "Senior leaders must immediately express candor, remorse, and a commitment to change in a high-profile setting—and make it sincere."[3]

PricewaterhouseCoopers (PwC) enjoys a stellar reputation, enhanced by its role calculating the winners of the Academy Awards. In 2017, though, it made a big mistake, in front of the world. The presenters for that year's Oscar for Best Picture were handed the wrong envelope and thus gave the award to the wrong film.[4] Confusion ensued backstage as the *La La Land* team mounted the stage and began acceptance speeches. After a hasty announcement that the actual winner was the film *Moonlight*, the *La La Land* producers handed over the award and returned to their seats.

PwC apologized swiftly and clearly. That night, it issued the following statement:

> We sincerely apologize to "Moonlight," "La La Land," Warren Beatty, Faye Dunaway, and Oscar viewers for the error that was made during the award announcement for Best Picture. The presenters had mistakenly been given the wrong category envelope and when discovered, was immediately corrected. We are currently investigating how this could have happened, and deeply regret that this occurred.
>
> We appreciate the grace with which the nominees, the Academy, ABC, and Jimmy Kimmel handled the situation.[5]

The statement was quick, acknowledged responsibility, apologized, and explained steps it was taking to avoid the mistake in the future. My only qualm about the statement is that slip into passive voice—"The presenters had mistakenly been given the wrong category envelope" would be improved if it read, "We mistakenly gave the presenters the wrong category envelope." Otherwise, though, this appears to be a textbook example of a good apology. In contrast, when Facebook attempted to mitigate the furor after it was revealed that it had shared fifty million users' personal data with Cambridge Analytica, a political consulting firm, CEO Mark Zuckerberg's public statements that failed to take responsibility (by not using the words "sorry" or "apologize" and appearing to deflect blame) prolonged and exacerbated the scandal.[6]

So, if your organization has done something that harmed others, should it issue an apology? Yes—but only if you can make it a good one. Sincere remorse is essential. Researchers studied twenty-nine videos of CEOs who apologized for corporate errors. They found that when the CEO smiled or otherwise looked happy during the apology, or even appeared neutral, the stock price dropped following the apology. When the CEO appeared sincerely remorseful, though, the company's stock price rose following the apology.[7] Where the CEO takes responsibility and appears regretful, customers rate the company more favorably and are inclined to forgive.

Organizations are sometimes uncomfortable issuing apologies due to the fear of litigation. If we apologize, the thinking goes, we've admitted we were at fault. They can sue us and we'll already have admitted liability. The only question will be how much we owe them.

This is certainly a consideration, and any corporate team will want to have a full discussion among leadership, including counsel, before issuing a statement that accepts responsibility and apologizes for misconduct. There is ample reason to believe, though, that a sincere and thoughtful apology is the safest route to minimize legal risk as well.[8] A study of medical procedures with adverse outcomes found that apology alone resolved 43 percent of cases with medical error and significantly reduced the time to resolve the claim.[9] When the University of Michigan moved to an open-disclosure, apology, and recompense model in response to medical errors instead of the traditional litigation model, litigation costs dropped by more than half, the average time to process claims fell from more than twenty months to about eight months, and insurance reserves fell by two-thirds.[10] Research has shown that people sue to understand what happened, to protect others, and to ensure that caregivers are accountable for their actions.[11] If that can be achieved by sharing information, accepting responsibility, and making amends, lawsuits may be avoided altogether.

# STEP FOUR

## EMPOWER

Leaders are those who empower others.
— BILL GATES

# Introduction

A s those who have suffered a trauma work to recover from its effects, we can help them by providing them with resources. The goal is to empower them to take the steps they need to heal, whether that is contacting security or counseling, accessing flexible work options, or reaching out for social services. Managers and all those who work with or are responsible for others should be aware of certain types of services available at their workplace or in the community. This section discusses some of the resources that are helpful to know about and where to find others when we need them. As we provide these resources, we should remember our limitations and not try to take over for the person in trouble—our role is to support them on their path, not to walk it for them.

IT BEGAN WITH a phone call from a credit card company.[1] Amy didn't have a credit card with that company, so she initially thought the call was a hoax. She checked the number and learned that it was in fact the number for the company's fraud department. What she learned on that call sent her through a multiyear morass of administrative and legal woes.

A stranger had used Amy's identity to apply for a card. Suspicious, the credit card company contacted Amy to verify her information. Amy was able to shut down that application, but when she contacted the credit reporting bureaus, she found that she was unable to answer the security questions they posed to allow her access to her account—because the identity thief's information had supplanted her own on her credit history. When she was finally able to access a report from one bureau, she learned that the thief had attempted to open more than fifty accounts with Amy's information, in just six months.

Thus began a lengthy journey to disentangle the mess the thief had made of Amy's financial life. To obtain her credit reports with the other two bureaus, she had to prove that she was in fact the real Amy. She mailed them copies of her birth certificate, social security card, and utility bills. Once she had all of the reports and a full list of the applications created and pending, she then placed fraud alerts with each of the credit reporting bureaus and froze her accounts. Amy had to file a police report and obtain an affidavit from the Federal Trade Commission, then contact each of the companies that had created an account or received an application from the thief—credit card companies, utilities, even a newspaper subscription. Each company had different requirements to sort through. One was a medical collection agency, which placed particularly onerous requirements due to HIPAA. And as Amy worked through each, some of the companies sent the debts created by the thief to collections agencies, creating another layer of bureaucracy for Amy to confront. Meanwhile, the thief was still applying for credit with Amy's name. It became like Whac-A-Mole to clear up the fraudulent accounts and bat down the new ones. Amy began a spreadsheet to track the information that was requested of her and what she'd provided, which eventually grew to more than two hundred entries.

Those who've been the victim of an identity theft must very quickly become experts in identity theft. On average, victims of identity theft will spend six months and between a hundred and two hundred hours cleaning up their credit[2]—and many spend much, much more.

Identity theft victims are not the only ones who have to undertake heroic efforts to recover from a crime. Someone assaulted or hit by a driver under the influence may have ongoing medical issues as well as bills to manage. Victims of domestic violence and stalking have to mask their locations, and sometimes their identities. Victims of revenge porn can spend untold hours working to find and remove illicit content online. Victims of environmental disasters may need to abandon their homes and undergo extensive medical monitoring. And victims of all types of wrongs may suffer mental health effects that require years of counseling.

We cannot do this work for them. But we can help. How? We can help by giving them resources. We help by empowering them to take the steps they need to take to begin the journey to healing and giving them some of the tools they'll need along the way.

# Why We Empower

A s discussed in Chapter Four, those in trauma may be having trouble accessing the complex planning part of their brains.[1] The situations they are in can be difficult enough, as they face the physical, financial, and emotional effects of what they've endured. The impact of trauma on the brain can exacerbate those feelings of being overwhelmed and make it seem impossible to move forward. We can help them navigate the thicket of responding to the traumatic event and get onto the path to healing by offering resources and other assistance.

The goal in providing assistance is to help them take the steps that they want to take. The best place to start is, "How can I help?" or "Tell me what you need." Perhaps the person knows exactly what he needs ("I want to take a two-week leave of absence") and you can either provide the resource yourself or direct him to someone who can ("Reach out to Jamal in HR"). If you ask the question, you allow him to direct his own recovery and ask for the things that he wants. It may take a moment, so give him some time to think. He may not know, of course. If that is the case, then you can offer a few suggestions.

If you have responsibility for others in your work, it is important to know some basic information about where those individuals can go if they need help. Thus, if you have employees who work for you, you should know where in your organization an employee can go for counseling services. If you are a human resources professional, you should know what security options are available in your office building. If you are a teacher or college professor, you should know what to do if students disclose that they're being bullied. This is not only for employees or colleagues, though. If you are a customer service representative, a doctor, or anyone who works with members of the public, it would be wise to know some basic information about resources that are available for those who have been victimized. In this section, I set forth the general types of services that it is helpful to know about, and where to find more when you need it. You can download a one-page list of resources on my website, www.blackbird-dc.com.

Another benefit of this part of the process is that it moves the conversation toward next steps. The speaker has shared something difficult; you have listened and acknowledged appropriately, then shared the information you can share. At some point, the conversation will need to be brought to a graceful end. Directing the person to resources outside of the room is a good way to begin that transition.

One final point. This step is one that I consider equally important for both the person in trauma and the person seeking to help. The reason is that it is essential when helping others that we recognize the limits of what we can do. Our role is to support the person but not to take over.

Helping someone in need can be immensely gratifying. Thus, it may be tempting to go further than simply providing information about where to find a resource. You may think, "Wouldn't it be even more helpful if I made that call for them?"

I would encourage you to resist that urge. As discussed in Step Three, one of the hardest things about being a victim is the loss of control. If we take away from those victimized the choice to take the steps to heal from what has happened to them, we are removing an important source of autonomy. In addition, if someone is not ready to take those steps to obtain help, our efforts will be wasted, and possibly even damaging. A domestic violence victim may not be ready to leave. As much as you may want to protect her, you cannot get her out of a situation if she is not ready to get out of it. Further, if you push too hard, she may feel ashamed that she is not following through on your suggestions and then avoid coming to you in the future. She will have lost an important ally at a time when she needs all the allies she can get.[2] It may be difficult, but as much as possible, provide the resources and then let go of the outcome. Allow the person in trauma to decide when, or whether, to follow up and seek the help you've identified. That way, when she is ready, the resource will actually be helpful.[3]

# Security Issues

Security truly is everyone's responsibility. If you cover the front desk, if you answer the phone sometimes, if you oversee a staff of three hundred, or sit in a cubicle along with fifteen coworkers, you should know what security resources are available and what emergency procedures are in place.

Does your organization have a security officer? Make sure that you know who that person is and how to reach him. If your organization doesn't have one, how about the building where you work? It is generally incredibly easy to find out security information, but if you wait until you need it, you may have waited too long. In addition, most people know about 911, but it's also important to know about 311. That's another way to reach law enforcement, when you have a concern about something that doesn't rise to the level of an emergency.

Once you have the information about security options available, pass it along:

- When your colleague mentions that her husband had a rough night and she is scared to go home
- When there's a weird package in the mailroom
- When a customer threatens to punch an employee

Or really, anytime issues of safety arise. Err on the side of caution. No one will criticize you for overreacting, but it can be devastating to miss the opportunity to head off an act of violence.

Security issues may not always be obvious to those experiencing them. A friend once told me that her ex-boyfriend was behaving in ways that were a little concerning. They had broken up months before, but he had recently sent a package to her home with a gift and a long letter about their time together. He texted her with increasing frequency, and though she tried to be clear that she did not want to reinitiate their relationship, she also found herself placating him because when she didn't respond to his texts, or did so tersely, she was met with a barrage of lengthy messages with accusations and pleas for responses. He worked near her office, and she kept running into him as she went to and from work—so often that she wondered if he was waiting for her. Once, as she sat at an outdoor café for lunch, he sat on a bench nearby, where he could see her. He was a law enforcement officer and always carried a gun.

As we discussed how she should handle his texts, and what she should do when she saw him, I asked if she had talked to her office's front desk security team. Her head cocked to one side. "Why?"

I reflected back what I'd heard from her. He had become increasingly agitated and demanding of her time. He had a gun and was possibly stalking her. "Isn't it conceivable that the security officers might respond differently if they knew that the man pacing in front of the building was armed and fixated on a woman inside?" She agreed that it was.

The security officer she spoke with was supportive and calm. He was glad that she came to him. He asked for a photo of the ex-boyfriend and confidentially distributed it to the rest of the security team. A few months later and without incident, the ex-boyfriend got another job and moved away. I don't know if he ever would have done anything dangerous. I do know, though, that ensuring that the security office had the information they needed allowed them to be prepared and gave my friend some much-needed peace of mind.

# Counseling

According to the 2017 National Study of Employers, 75 percent of employers provide Employee Assistance Programs (EAPs) to help employees with personal issues that may impact their life or work.[1] For large employers, the figure is above 90 percent.[2] EAPs can help with anything from mental health issues to alcoholism and addiction to marital challenges to disputes between coworkers to financial or legal concerns.[3] The services they provide are free to employees and, often, their family members. Despite that, though, only about 7 percent of employees make use of their EAP.[4] This is generally due to a lack of information about the services that EAP provides and how to access them.[5]

Break the mold! EAP can be a fantastic resource, both to provide counseling directly or to refer employees to outside low-cost assistance. Their services are confidential. Encourage others to make use of EAP in appropriate circumstances. In addition, your office human resources personnel can assist with accessing resources, whether EAP or other services.

What about when EAP is not available? Perhaps the person who needs help is not an employee but rather a member of the public, or maybe EAP is not offered at your organization. There are still options for referring someone to free or low-cost help. Do you know about 211? Dial 911 for emergencies, 311 for nonemergency police assistance, and 211 for referrals to community organizations.[6] Callers can reach specialists who can refer to local resources for:

- Crisis intervention
- Support groups
- Counseling
- Transportation
- Family assistance like adult day care
- Protective services
- Financial assistance

And more.[7] Finally, there are national hotlines and online resources that are available seven days a week, twenty-four hours a day. These include:

- Crisis textline: 741741
- National Suicide Prevention Lifeline: 1-800-273-TALK (800-273-8255) (Spanish: 888-628-9454)[8]
- National Domestic Violence Hotline: 800–799–7233 (TTY 800-787-3224)
- National Sexual Assault Hotline: 800-656-HOPE (4673)
- LGBTQ National Helpline: 888-843-4564
- National Substance Abuse and Mental Health Services Administration: 800-662-HELP (4357) (TTY 800-662-4889)
- Disaster Distress Helpline (for those dealing with the aftermath of natural or human-caused disasters like hurricanes, floods, wildfires, tornadoes, earthquakes, and mass violence): 800-985-5990

It's helpful to keep this list handy; consider marking this page so that you can come back to it when you need it. On my website, www.blackbird-dc .com, you can download a one-page list of resources to keep on your desk. By equipping people with resources, we show that they are not alone. There are resources out there to help. In addition, directing them to services demonstrates that we care about them and want them to get the help they need.

# Flexible Work Options

Emma, a lawyer,[1] was a highly regarded specialist in her field when she learned that she had breast cancer. The chemotherapy she needed once a week was at a hospital near her house. The sessions were early in the morning, and afterward she was tired. She asked her supervisor if she could telework on treatment days rather than commute into the office. He refused, without explanation or any investigation into the options available. Unsurprisingly, she finished the chemotherapy, recovered, and within a year had found a new job.

Flexible work policies can mean the difference between an employee who can continue working through a difficult time and one who ends up leaving his company. They also can build, or destroy, loyalty. If you are in charge of employees, it would be helpful to know what policies your organization has that cover time away from work, and under what circumstances.

The options may include:

- *Leave.* Most workplaces have some form of leave policy that covers illness and bereavement. It is worthwhile to understand the parameters of those policies. Can coworkers donate leave? Are there special leave policies for those caring for a family member or those experiencing domestic violence?

- *Flextime.* Some employees benefit from the ability to shift their work schedules. This may allow them, for instance, to finish work early in the afternoon so they can care for a sick relative in the evenings. Managers should understand what is possible and consider whether a flexible schedule would be feasible, even temporarily.

- *Telework.* The quarantines required by the coronavirus taught us that telework can be used much more widely. Situational telework can make a difference for those going through a challenging time. An employee who is being stalked, for instance, may no longer feel safe coming into the same work location every day. A period of telework may ease his mind and increase his security—as well as that of others in the office.

- *Part-time.* An employee may wish to work part-time for a while as she struggles to recover from a traumatic event. If she does so, is she guaranteed her full-time job when she is ready to return?

A thorough understanding of the rules around flexible work can allow you to advocate for your employees as they go through difficult periods. Your human resources officials should be able to assist you and your employees with understanding the options.

# Other Community Services

O f course, there are myriad other services that an employee or member of the public may need. He's concerned that someone in his church is a trafficking victim; she's lost her retirement savings in a Ponzi scheme; their Social Security numbers have been published online. People may need referrals for concerns about elder abuse, revenge porn, or miscarriage. They may need help with byzantine insurance requirements or a short-term loan to get them through the holidays. You can't be an expert in everything. Fortunately, you don't have to be.

You only need 211.

Similar to 411, the number for information, 211 is a service call center. When you dial the number, you are routed to the local or regional center, which is staffed by specialists who have access to a vast database of agencies and community aid organizations. They can provide you with information on the relevant service or connect you directly. It's available in all fifty states of the United States, and in Canada.[1]

You don't need to be an expert in all of the resources out there. Just direct them to 211.

# STEP FIVE

## RETURN

Great is the art of beginning, but greater is the art of ending.
—HENRY WADSWORTH LONGFELLOW

# Introduction

The final step of LASER is to return—return to the person in trauma and return to yourself. The way we end an interaction can color our perception of the entire interaction. Therefore, it's worthwhile to end on a positive note. For the person in trauma, this means a graceful, easy exit from the conversation with reminders of our tasks, to show that we will not forget about him as soon as he walks out the door. Then, later on, we return to him to check in and see if he needs additional resources or information. For us, return means that we close the conversation well, take notes and set reminders to follow up, and then, most importantly, we take care of ourselves. We recognize the impact of hearing a difficult story and we allow ourselves the time and support we need to process it. This section of the book covers all of these, as well as providing more ideas for how to create a workplace that is open to receiving and handling stories of difficulty.

ONCE I SAT on a plane next to an empty seat. We were getting close to the time for takeoff, and I thought maybe I was going to get to stretch out a little. Instead, just before the doors closed, a woman hustled down the aisle. She was carrying too many bags and had trouble managing them. She seemed flustered. She was also grumbling, the whole way down the aisle, about the service on these airlines, how narrow the aisles were, how late she was, and how this was all ridiculous.

Of course, she was heading for me. I hopped up and let her get herself situated. She continued grumbling as she organized her things, settled into her seat, and latched her seat belt.

I remained silent. When she finally looked over at me, I smiled. "Flying can be a pain," I commiserated.

"Ugh, you have no idea," she began. She launched into the early wake-up, the flight delay, the nearly missed connection, the bag that probably hadn't made it. I didn't say anything, just listened. Sometimes I smiled sympathetically.

Eventually, she began to run out of steam. She looked away, lips pursed. "I hate flying. It always scares me. My husband used to calm me down."

She paused. I sat with her in silence.

"He died a month ago," she said finally.

"I'm so sorry," I said. "What was he like?"

She told me about him. He sounded like a really good man. I was sorry that he had died. As she talked about him, her entire demeanor changed. She seemed younger, lighter, calmer, and happier.

It wasn't a long flight, and the time passed quickly as we chatted. The talk about her husband transitioned into talk about our jobs. We found out we had some things in common in our work lives, and we discussed those. She was happy to learn that I lived in Washington, DC. She loved DC, especially the museums, and she urged me to see her favorite sculpture at the National Gallery of Art.

Eventually, the captain announced our descent. My seatmate got a slightly panicked look. "Can I contact you? Can we stay in touch?"

Now, I am as paranoid as you can imagine someone who's worked with victims for twenty-five years would be. I have heard harrowing stories about stalking, identity theft, random violence, and more. I know that abusers can come in every shape and form, and I don't kid myself that I can keep myself safe.

I did a quick mental calculation. She seemed sane, despite her initial agitation. She had told me she lived in a different state. I felt wary about sharing my personal contact information with her, but I couldn't see any downsides to sharing my work information with her. At the Justice Department, they irradiate all packages, and there are security guards at the doors. The worst that could happen was that she'd call or email me a lot, but that seemed a long shot, and manageable if it happened. "Sure," I said, and fished a business card out of my bag.

She grew quiet, staring at the back of the seat in front of her as the plane sank beneath the clouds and toward the earth, gripping my card in both her hands.

It's hard to leave an intense conversation. The return to mundane concerns about scheduling and emails can feel jarring. For those who've had the opportunity to discuss something difficult, it can be much harder. So few people allow them to do it. It's important, then, to end a conversation gently, and respectfully.

In fact, research has shown that the way we leave a situation can impact our memory of the entire experience. A bad ending can taint our recollection of an otherwise pleasant experience, and a good one can rescue a terrible one. In an experiment, test subjects had to hold their hands in cold water for one minute. Sometimes, the experiment ended there, and sometimes the subjects had to follow that with submerging their hands in slightly warmer water for an additional thirty seconds. Oddly, the subjects preferred the second experiment, which prolonged the painful experience.[1] Ending with a slightly better (though still unpleasant) experience colored their perception of the entire event.[2] Positive experiences are colored similarly. When test subjects were given pieces of candy that were particularly exciting followed by ones that were fine but less exciting (a full-size Hershey bar followed by a piece of gum), they rated their experience less favorably than when they weren't given the second piece of candy at all.[3]

Thus, it is important for us to think through how we end any interaction or experience, but particularly a challenging one. You've worked so hard to establish trust throughout the conversation. A goodbye that feels like a brush-off can taint the entire conversation and make it less likely that the person will open up to you in the future or come back to you for more information or resources when needed. In this section, I discuss the final step of the LASER technique, return—how to end the conversation on a solid footing, come back later to check in, as well as how to return to yourself after a hard conversation.

By the way, my airplane seatmate never did show up at my work or call or email me. Months later, though, as I sorted through the papers on my desk, I came across a letter. It was from her. She'd sent a kind note thanking me for our conversation. She mentioned again the sculpture she loved. "It's a woman with a veil," she said. "Don't forget to go see it."

A few weeks later, I followed her advice. I wandered through the maze of rooms at the National Gallery of Art until I found the sculpture. Called *The Veiled Nun*, the marble bust is of a beautiful woman with a veil, thin as gossamer silk, resting lightly over her face. I thought of my seatmate and the way she'd transformed over the course of our conversation. Stress melted from her face as she recounted stories of her beloved husband. Her grief, it seems, was a thin layer obscuring the vibrant and fascinating woman beneath. I was glad that through our conversation I was able to see past it.

# Why We Return

When we reach the end of the conversation and have listened, acknowledged, and shared the information and resources we can share, we may feel that we've done all there is to do. There is one more step to take, though. It is important that we end the conversation well and that we leave the door open to future interactions on the subject. We should provide some method for the person to get back in touch with us to ask further questions or learn about developments, and it is also wise to return to the person to follow up later. Here's why.

First, it may be difficult for the person to understand and retain the information we've shared. Make it easy for her to come back to you when she's forgotten what you said about how to apply for part-time status or whom to contact in EAP. You don't want the information you've provided to go to waste because the person was not in a good frame of mind to retain it.

In addition, when you later follow up with her, you can assess how the person is doing. Does she seem happy and able to focus on work? Is she instead flustered, depressed, or anxious? By checking in, you have the opportunity to find out whether the resources you provided were helpful and offer any additional services needed. You can also provide an update on your own efforts and on the status of any ongoing investigation.

Returning to the person is not solely about sharing additional information, though. It's also important because it communicates to the person that you will not disappear once she leaves the room. She may have shared something quite personal with you and feel vulnerable. Don't breach the trust that you've built up through the conversation by vanishing or failing to follow through on your commitments. This is a show of respect—she wasn't wrong to trust you. You weren't simply saying what you needed to say to get her out of the room. You take seriously what she said and will continue to be a resource for her.

Finally, this last step of the LASER method is not solely about returning to the person in trauma. We also need to return to ourselves. We must check in with our own feelings and give ourselves the support we need. Listening is not easy. Compassion fatigue can creep up on us and affect our work, our relationships, and our health. To continue to be of service to others, we have to take care of ourselves, as well.

# Prepare to Exit the Conversation

The first step in ending the conversation gracefully is to provide some warning. You don't want to spring on someone that her time is up; instead, let her know with five or ten minutes left that the interaction will soon be coming to an end. This avoids a startling end or giving the person the feeling of being unceremoniously dropped.

It helps to interject yourself a bit more than you likely have been doing. As you've been acknowledging what she's told you and sharing information, you've been talking more than you did when the person first shared her story, but it's possible that she has been talking a fair amount as well. This is normal: you acknowledge something, and the person sees that you are open to hearing from her, so she shares a little more. You acknowledge that and begin to share information, then she mentions something else or asks a question or tells you about a book she's read on this topic. Conversations are dynamic and can't be overly scripted. Eventually, though, you need to wind down the discussion, and that requires you to assert a bit more control.

Sometimes, it's easy. You both realize that the conversation is winding down, so with subtle body language—a shift forward in your seat, a glance at your watch or at the door—you can signal to the person that it's time to move on. The person will say, "I should probably get going," or "I'm sure you've got other people waiting." It's important to do this at a time when the conversation has already slowed some or else when you yourself are speaking. The goal is not to appear bored by what's being said. Usually, this is not hard to finesse, as most people sense that they have already had a good amount of your time and will be looking for any signs that you need to move on.

Some people, though, will need a bit more. They are so glad that they've found someone willing to sit and stay present with them in their grief that they don't want to let that person go. They'll keep repeating what they've said, or adding little details that aren't really helpful. If you leave any room in the conversation, they'll fill it.

Resist the urge to cut off the conversation abruptly with a "Well, I've got to go now." A harsh leaving can sully all that you've been able to do to help the person throughout the conversation.

Instead, give plenty of warning. If you've set an expectation early in the conversation about the amount of time you have available, now is the time to remind them of that. Wait for a quieter, less intense moment. Then, gently, "It's getting close to that noon meeting I have. I'll have to get going soon." Or, "I've got to leave in about ten minutes." Or, "My next appointment is coming in just a bit."

What if you don't have another appointment? You can talk for as long as you like, of course, but I would urge you to watch for when your attention is flagging. You may find your empathy starting to dip. "She already said that," you'll think. Or, "He's being a little whiny." It's okay to feel that way; no one has an infinite supply of patience. Just notice that it's happening, so that you can take the steps to end the conversation before that feeling seeps out and things start to sour. It's also not helpful to the other person for you to carry on the conversation indefinitely. You need to end it at some point. It's best to do it while you both have good energy and feel the conversation has been productive.

Don't make up an appointment—doing so would be a breach of the trust you've worked so hard to establish. Instead, say something along the lines of, "I am going to need to get back to work in a few minutes." "I have a few other things on my desk that I'll need to turn to soon." "I have to get going soon."

Next, give her a chance to say anything more she wants to say, now that she understands your time limits. "Is there anything else you want me to know before I go?" "Have we covered the things you wanted to cover?" "What else?"

In my experience, people usually don't come up with anything new to say at this point in the conversation, but offering up the opportunity to say more gives them a minute to assess whether they feel the conversation is complete. Usually, they realize that it is and that they've said all they wanted to say. Sometimes, they'll say something more, but most people understand the limit you've just set on your time and make a last point or two quickly. Rarely, you may need a second gentle reminder—"I have to go in just a minute," or "I'm about out of time, unfortunately, and there are just a few more things I want to go over." Then you can move on to discussing any next steps.

# Remind of Next Steps

Now that the person has had a chance to say all that he wanted to say, and has realized that he has, it's easier for you to shift to next steps. If you've been taking notes, this is a good time to review them for any tasks that either of you has agreed to take on. This will help make sure nothing falls through the cracks. You can remind him of the process. This is also a nice time to thank him again. "Thanks for coming to me with this. I'll check in with Linda and Malcolm, see if there is anyone else I need to talk to, then write up a report and send it on to Glen." Or, "Remember to get in your statement to Lee by Friday." Be specific if you can, but if not, vague is okay: "Thanks for the information. I'll follow up, and this will be really useful as I do."

This step is practical and helpful. Over the course of the conversation, you've learned things, and so have they. You likely each have next steps to take. Reminding you both of these steps helps to set them in your minds. For those who've been through a traumatic event, this is especially important, as the swirl of emotions they're experiencing makes it harder to process information and remember it later. If possible, write down any steps they need to take and hand it to them.

Even beyond the usefulness of this reminder in practical terms, though, setting forth the list of tasks signals forcefully that this conversation will end. We will leave this room, and then additional steps will be taken outside, later. This prepares the person for the ending and fortifies them in knowing that, though the conversation is nearly over, more will happen.

Once you've covered these practical issues, it's good to check in with the person. "How are you doing now?" "That was a lot, I know. How are you feeling?" This reminds the person to check in with himself—how is he actually doing? You have now given him a chance to discuss something difficult and supported him with acknowledgment, shared information, and told him about resources. His mind may be reeling. He may be feeling tired, overwhelmed, relieved, anxious, or any number of other emotions. Giving him just a moment to reflect on and acknowledge those feelings helps to leave the interaction on a positive note. You can then validate what he's expressed: "I'll bet. I'd be exhausted too." "That makes perfect sense."

The check-in also gives him a chance to ask for something more or different if he needs it. He may say, "I'm still feeling kind of anxious about whether you're going to tell people what I said. Can you go through the rules around that again?" You don't want to leave any stone unturned. The two of you are in that moment, right then. Take care of the issues that have come up. If things are allowed to linger, they will only get worse. Better to hear what is still troubling the person so that it can be addressed in whatever way is appropriate.

# Follow Up

Eventually, the conversation will be over and the person will leave. You will make any notes you need to make, send any emails, or apprise others as necessary. Then your role will be finished. Right?

Years ago, I myself was the victim of a crime. Our next-door neighbor was not a stable man. He was sometimes aggressive toward my wife and me with little or no provocation. We lived in rowhouses, in very close proximity. One day, my wife was in front of our house with our toddler, who was drawing on the sidewalk with chalk. The neighbor became convinced that our toddler had drawn a line on the sidewalk in front of his house, and he became irate. He began screaming at them until they rushed into the house and locked the door. He then took the chalk they'd abandoned and wrote a homophobic slur in huge letters in front of our house, while continuing to shout threats. When a passerby confronted him, the neighbor began throwing punches.

We called the police. Officers arrived quickly and removed him from the property. He spent the night in jail and was going to be released the next day. He was never ultimately charged with a crime. That was fine with me; I simply wanted him to stop being aggressive, which he did. What made a difference to me, though, was that the officers did not simply move on to the next case. They followed up the next day to let me know that he was going to be released. They called again a few days afterward to see if we were having any further problems. They made clear that they wanted to hear of any future incidents and gave me the direct number for the officer to call.

Those extra steps were the difference between feeling like a number and feeling like a person. We felt supported during something that was scary and upsetting.

Once someone has come to you for support during a difficult time, it is important not to drop him when your interaction with him is over. Showing him that you continue to care is an essential part of enhancing his trust of you and the organization. Giving him a way to contact you is one piece of this, but you reaching out affirmatively is also important. A check-in shows that you are not blowing him off and that you continue to be there for him if he needs it. In fact, studies have shown that for those who are suicidal, a follow-up thirty days after the suicidal moment reduces the rate of later suicide attempts.[1] Even for those with less severe difficulties, a later check-in builds trust and a sense of safety.

This can be done in a number of different ways, depending on what is right for the situation and your relationship:

- *A follow-up email*, once you've identified additional information, may be appropriate. This could be to provide the contact information for the security office, what you've learned about where complaints should be sent, or a brief follow-up to remind him of next steps.
- *An in-person check-in*, when possible, can be really effective. The check-in can be brief or more extensive. A brief check-in is intended to show your ongoing concern and availability. It also gives you a chance to assess for yourself how he's doing and to offer again any assistance you can provide. "How are things going with your

mom?" "I hope you're feeling better. I've been thinking about you and all you're going through." If the person has more to discuss, you have opened the door for that. If not, he knows that you continue to be a resource. It is wise, of course, to do a check-in along these lines when you are not in front of other people, so that the person does not have to answer questions from others that he is not prepared to answer ("Why? What's going on with your mom?").

- *A more formal follow-up* may sometimes be necessary. Perhaps you've agreed to advise the person of the outcome of further investigation or to follow up with information from another department. It's important to honor that commitment. If you have specified a certain day for follow-up, do your best to meet that deadline or at least to touch base and explain why you will not be able to. Remember that the goal is not to fritter away all of the trust and goodwill you've built. Even absent a specific commitment, keep the person apprised of any developments that may affect him. Again, your goal is to ensure that you are seen as a reliable source of information, so that he does not turn to other sources, like office gossip or conjecture. If he knows that you will keep him in the loop, he will rely on you for information, which helps to ensure that the information that gets passed along is accurate.

There is one caveat to the subsequent check-in, though. As you follow up, be mindful of whether your presence reminds the person of the traumatic incident. A Title IX officer, for instance, may be indelibly connected in a student's mind with the assault that she reported. In that situation, it would be wise to ask the student how she would prefer a follow-up. For highly sensitive situations, I often suggest that the person in trauma set up a separate email address for communications regarding the difficult event, which she can access when she chooses. That helps to ensure that she isn't blindsided with a reminder of the traumatic event in the middle of an otherwise good day.

# A Return to Yourself

R eturning is not only important for the person we've supported. It's also important that we return to ourselves. Compassion fatigue is a common side effect of supporting others through challenging times. It can affect our physical and mental health, our work, and our relationships. To guard against it, we must maintain a healthy respect for our boundaries and take care of ourselves both during and after the conversation.

## Our Power, and Our Limits

Kelsey Smith graduated from Shawnee Mission West High School in Overland Park, Kansas, in May 2007. Kelsey was known for her big heart and her care for those around her: she was the one who always showed up with balloons for friends' birthdays, she was an amazing big sister to her younger brother, and she made drawings of their pets for family members whose dogs had died.[1] A creative artist and a talented musician, she planned to play clarinet in the marching band at the University of Kansas that fall.

Nine days into her summer vacation, Kelsey went to Target to get a gift for her boyfriend, John, for their six-month anniversary. She spoke with her mother as she was checking out and told her she was heading home. It was 7:00 p.m. At seven thirty, she was to meet John at her house, an eight-minute ride away. She never arrived.[2]

John called and texted her repeatedly but couldn't reach her. After thirty minutes, he reached out to Kelsey's father, Greg Smith, a law enforcement officer. Greg began calling area police departments and hospitals. No one could find Kelsey. Hours later, they discovered her abandoned car across the street from the Target.[3]

Kelsey's mother, Missey, called the family's cell phone provider to ask them to ping Kelsey's phone in the hopes that it would lead them to Kelsey. The provider refused. Greg later called and asked as well. The provider still refused. It refused again when a local police officer on the case requested, and even when the district attorney's office issued a subpoena.[4]

Meanwhile, days passed. As Missey later said, "What does a parent go through when a child is missing? You don't eat because you don't know if your child is eating. You don't sleep, because you wonder if they are sleeping. It is pure hell."[5]

Finally, after four long days, the cell phone company provided the location of the cell tower where Kelsey's cell phone had last pinged. Within forty-five minutes, searchers found Kelsey's body.[6]

As they fought through their grief, Greg and Missey decided to honor their daughter's life by focusing on what Kelsey would want. "Make a difference" became their motto. Frustrated that cell service providers weren't required to cooperate with law enforcement in matters of life and death, they lobbied their state legislature to change the law. The Kelsey Smith Act is now the law in twenty-five states.[7]

One of the first places it made a difference was in the Smiths' home state of Kansas. Soon after Kelsey's Law passed, a car was stolen with an infant in the back seat. Because the mother's phone was still in the front seat, law enforcement was able to find the car and recover the baby within an hour. Through tears, Missey said, "That baby is home and alive because my baby isn't. Kelsey really is making a difference."[8]

Those who have been victimized can do incredible things. I am astonished, over and over again, by the way that people take their grief and integrate it into a stronger, fuller life, for themselves and for all of us, in so many different ways.

They create incredible works of art, like the survivors of war and ethnic cleansing who sew story cloths, tapestries that recount their experiences of genocide and sexual violence.[9] These cloths stand as beautiful testaments to their healing. Leilani Schweitzer, whose son Gabriel died as a result of a medical error, poured herself into creating bright and colorful art installations after losing her son. "My art saved my life after Gabriel died," she says.[10]

Many who've undergone difficult events use their experience to help others. Shari Kastein escaped an abusive relationship with her fifteen-month-old daughter but ended up homeless and living in her car. Kastein relied on a battered women's shelter to knit her life back together. Once she was back on her feet, she began to invite other victims of abuse to stay in her apartment. Eventually, she founded a Family Crisis Center. Over the following thirty-four years of aiding others, her work has grown to cover seventeen counties and serve more than a thousand people annually. Kastein has worked to develop a domestic and sexual violence helpline, and placed victim advocates in community health centers across the seventeen counties to allow for a discreet way for victims to seek aid.[11]

At a training I gave, a woman said, "I am the HR manager at my company. A coworker came to me and told me that her supervisor raped her. I listened and I believed her. I asked what she wanted to have happen, and I tried to give her everything she wanted, if I could. I provided her with resources for support services. I checked in with her again and again. But still, she spiraled downward. She got really depressed. She started missing work. She just seemed to slip away. What else could I have done?"

I wish I had the answer to that. I wish that I could give you the book, the adage, the resource that would take away the pain from someone who's been hurt. There is no easy solution, of course. We are so limited, and yet so powerful. What we must do, the only thing we can do, is sit with the person through their pain.

It may take a long time. It may, in fact, take forever. The reality is that the person you knew before may be forever altered by the experience. As she begins to integrate what happened into the rest of her life, though, a new person may emerge—someone who is stronger, wiser, who cries more easily but also laughs more. Trust that this experience, as painful as it is, is not the end of her story. What she experiences today will not be her experience in five years.

And who knows what those years will hold? If we try to take over, we rob people of the path that they have before them. That path may be so much bigger, richer, fuller, than anything we could have dreamed.

## Taking Care of Ourselves

Thus, the final part of the LASER process is a return to ourselves. We must recognize that it is not easy to support someone through a difficult time. Exposure to trauma, whether in one instance or over time, can affect us. As recounted in the *Atlantic Monthly*, one counselor noted that after working with abuse victims, "she started to view formerly benign settings as possibly threatening, and she found it hard to maintain her normally upbeat attitude."[12] A review of case workers providing community mental health services found that nearly one in five had symptoms of posttraumatic stress disorder. A study of therapists working with survivors of sexual abuse found that almost half of them had secondary trauma.[13]

It's not only therapists and case workers who experience secondary trauma. I worked with a man at the Justice Department who prosecuted child exploitation cases. He was gentle and kind, thoughtful and smart. He did incredible work and protected so many kids. We worked on a project together for a few years, and I always enjoyed talking with him. Our paths didn't cross for a bit, and then we were brought together on another project. This time, he seemed like a different person—more caustic, bitter, sarcastic, and prone to anger. I was shocked at the transformation. Eventually, I realized that he was likely experiencing the effects of secondary trauma, or compassion fatigue, from his years working on those brutal cases. He transferred away from the child exploitation section soon after. In fact, studies have shown that lawyers working with those in trauma have higher levels of compassion fatigue than mental health professionals, likely because their profession does not have a culture of discussing difficult experiences.[14]

Secondary trauma is common in those who work with people experiencing trauma, from nurses and physicians to aid workers to lawyers to first responders to therapists to human resource professionals and more. It can develop following one traumatic event or multiple traumas across months or years. It shows up in a myriad of physical, mental, and emotional effects, including trouble sleeping, anxiety, anger, sadness, fatigue, a sense of isolation, helplessness, rigid thinking, apathy or numbness, guilt, appetite changes, hypervigilance, and a weakened immune system.[15] It can impact our productivity, our relationships, our judgment, and our health.[16]

The tricky thing about compassion fatigue is that it usually develops slowly over time. I was able to see it starkly in my former coworker because I hadn't seen him in a few years. It's harder to recognize it happening to those we see every day and harder still to recognize it in ourselves. So how do we guard against it? As in much of life, the best defense is a good offense. Preventing the trauma from seeping in is the best option, if you can do it.

The best protections against secondary trauma are healthy boundaries and ongoing maintenance. Having healthy boundaries means recognizing the limits of what you can provide. Don't take on the role of fixing the problem or holding up another person all by yourself. What we can do is important, but limited. Recognize those limits and let go of what you have no power to change. In particular, do not tie your own happiness to someone else's recovery. Those you are trying to help may reject your assistance outright, may begin to make progress and then fall backward, or start therapy or drug treatment and then quit. This is their path, not yours. You can help them along the way, but you can't walk it for them.

By ongoing maintenance, I mean take care of yourself. It is so easy to let this slide. We have so much to do. We minimize our own needs to take care of the myriad needs of the world around us. We're no good to the world around us, though, when we're depleted. Of course you know this, and of course you'll still ignore your needs, as do I. Here's what helps me:

- *Make it a routine.* Whatever your self-care is, make it as much a part of your morning or evening routine as brushing your teeth.

For me, I do a little yoga and meditation every morning after my shower. Yours could be a morning walk with the dog, playing the piano for thirty minutes after dinner, saying a prayer before going to bed, or anything else. The key is to make it an everyday occurrence, a habit, a promise.

• *Talk about the hard stuff.* I admit, I'm not good about this. I want to protect those around me from the weight of the stories I've heard. I tend to minimize or gloss over. I do this in kindness to my loved ones, but leaving all that sitting with me is not a kindness to them because of the way it makes an impact on me. I also do it because I don't want to admit that hearing hard stories affects me. I want to think that I am strong enough to shoulder the weight of those stories without strain. It is not true. I am not superhuman, and neither are you. We have to find ways to process those stories. Of course, we also have to respect confidentiality. Find someone you can tell—a friend, a colleague, your journal, a hotline if necessary—or talk about what is hard for you without describing the details or anything that would identify the people involved. Don't underestimate the benefits of therapy.

Despite our best efforts, sometimes compassion fatigue will creep in. Some stories will knock you sideways no matter how careful you are about boundaries and self-care. The important thing is to recognize it happening and address it. The earlier we catch it, the more easily it can be addressed. If we let it linger, it exacerbates and is harder to combat. The key is to identify your own warning signs.

The first sign is usually that you've started to drop your self-care routine. Suddenly, you don't have time for it, or it seems self-indulgent. *I'll get back to it when things ease up*, you think. That thought is the first indication that you need to double down on the self-care. A Zen proverb says, "You should sit in meditation for twenty minutes every day, unless you're too busy—then you should sit for an hour." If you're at all like me, you'll be really grumpy about this. You need to keep forcing yourself until you stop grousing about it.

Another sign of secondary trauma is that the things you love suddenly seem like a burden. For example, one of my favorite things is sharing a meal with friends. I love dinner parties and I love going out to restaurants with people I enjoy. I know that when I start to view dinner with friends with dread, as a chore instead of something I'm looking forward to, that's a sign that I'm getting burned out.

There are others, too, that are unique to each person. Know your warning signs. Maybe for you it's when you can't fall asleep at night, or you lose your appetite, or you find yourself craving a beer. If there is some addiction or unhealthy behavior that tends to haunt you, this is when it will pounce.

If you're lucky, when you miss those warning signs, a friend or loved one will point it out to you. "You seem really tired—is everything all right?" "We've missed you at the gym." Sometimes these aren't expressed with perfect care and empathy ("What's going on with you? You're so sensitive lately."), but try to recognize them as the help that they are—those around you identifying what you cannot. In the same way, it is helpful for you to speak up when you see others exhibiting the signs of secondary trauma. Find a gentle way to point it out to them, be a listening ear, and encourage self-care.

When you have gotten to the point of burnout, the way out is through the same steps as the prevention methods, but hit them harder. More of your self-care routine—longer walks, extra time with family, more rest. Lean into your faith, if that speaks to you. Therapy, again, can be a lifesaver. If not through talking, find some other way to process what's bothering you, perhaps through a creative art. It can help to keep a list of things that make you happy for those times when the world seems bleak. Finally, the most powerful mood shifter, as ample research shows, is gratitude.[17] A daily practice of noticing things you are fortunate to have in your life will pay off exponentially.

My final point on this is that you should be careful of the temptation to think of these steps as things that other people need, but not you. There is a hubris to the sentiment that you alone do not need self-care, support, and the opportunity to discuss difficult things with which you come into contact. You are human, with all of the strengths and weaknesses of our kind. Equally, you are no less worthy than all others; you deserve the same care and attention. You are entitled to the air you breathe, the space you take up in the world, and all that you need to feel whole and full in the world. And we need you whole and full, because there is much work to do.

# What Else We Can Do

**M**any have asked me what else they can do to show that they want to hear about the difficulties others are facing. In reality, once you have mastered these techniques, people will find you to share their stories. As I shared earlier, I am approached by strangers on airplanes, as well as by friends and, yes, coworkers. Encouraging people to open up is usually not the issue. There are a few things leaders can do, though, to encourage those they work with to bring up the issues that are troubling them so that they can be addressed.

## Talk About It

Be explicit with the people you lead and serve about not wanting the difficult issues buried. Look for an opportunity to mention it at a meeting or include it in a written communication. You can use this book as a jumping-off point.

"All, I just read a book on how we communicate about hard things, and I want you to know that I understand that we are all humans first, which means that, sometimes, life happens. If there is something challenging you, remember that there are fantastic resources out there—and right here—to help. We have counseling services, security, human resources, and a lot of other options. You are each a valued member of our team, and if you're struggling, we want to help, so please don't hesitate to reach out." A workplace session on domestic violence, suicide prevention, or the resources available through EAP can also demonstrate your commitment.

In addition, talk about issues of bias and harassment. Do this periodically, and not only in response to an issue in the news or at work. Don't assume that just because you haven't heard about a problem, it doesn't exist. Make it clear that bias and harassment are not tolerated, and tell people where to go to report it. Studies on bias and harassment training indicate that it is most effective when it includes an element of bystander intervention, so encourage others to report troubling conduct that they observe.[1]

## Enact Policies

If you are in a position to do so, enact or advocate for flexible work options, which can allow people to continue working during challenging periods. Flexible work options improve employee loyalty, productivity, operational costs, retention, and more.[2]

Other workplace policies can help as well. For instance, 65 percent of companies have no domestic violence policy covering issues like leave availability, telework options, and when a domestic violence victim should notify office security about a restraining order.[3] There are numerous sample policies available online that can be modified to your office's needs.

Policies around bias and harassment should be explicit regarding how reports are to be made and the consequences for violations. Ensure that complaints are handled quickly and that policies provide for frequent updates to those who file complaints.

Finally, make sure that policies are well publicized and followed. A policy that sits on a shelf until it is needed to defend a lawsuit is not serving your workforce.

# Model

Priya,[4] an assistant general counsel for a Fortune 500 company, leads a team of lawyers, paralegals, and support staff. Influenced by Chimimanda Adichie's TED Talk, "The Danger of a Single Story," she began her first meeting in her new role in the law department by inviting her team to spend twenty to thirty minutes discussing who they are. She started things off. To show that she invited more than a recitation of professional backgrounds, she discussed her own history as a child of immigrants and talked about losing her brother at an early age. Though some were reticent to open up, by the time the exercise made its way around the table, team members were discussing things like being the first in their family to go to college, illnesses, impactful spiritual travel, and more. Later, when Priya's mother passed away unexpectedly, she spoke frankly with her team about her grief and asked for the support she needed to manage her workload. Her model of dealing openly with challenges meant that her team has been strong enough to tackle staffing changes, unexpected case outcomes, and the upheaval caused by the pandemic and support one another through it all.

Being an empathetic leader means we have to do more than talk the talk. If we want our teams to know that it is truly safe to discuss the hard things, we have to show them. This means that we have to make ourselves vulnerable. We have to talk about the things we are struggling with, we have to admit our shortcomings, and we have to apologize when we make mistakes.

Creating an open work environment is not a one-step process. With leadership, commitment, training, and policies that both instruct and inspire, though, the rewards in trust, productivity, and loyalty will be significant.

# CONCLUSION

My wish for you is that you continue. Continue to be who and how you are,
to astonish a mean world with your acts of kindness.

— MAYA ANGELOU

# The Benefits of the LASER Method

LASER is thus five steps: Listen. Acknowledge. Share. Empower. Return. I have used these steps in a ten-minute conversation at the dog park and on a sleepless night with a suicidal friend. I have used them with my kids, a lot. They have guided me through challenging situations at work, from coming up with the agency response on what information we can share with victims of online child exploitation to how to support a colleague who was attacked in a meeting.

What I've gotten from the LASER steps is immense. Primarily, I've been able to help others. When we help others, we help ourselves. There is research to back this up,[1] but I'll bet you already knew that. I always try to remind myself, when I'm feeling down, that the best way to feel better is to find someone to help. Goodness knows there are plenty of people out there who need it.

Because of LASER, I have gotten to support friends, family members, and colleagues through some of their worst times. This has built for me strong ties with an amazing community of people. I have certainly leaned on them, as well. I have also laughed, danced, and shared meals with them. When you are there for the hard times, it can make the good times even sweeter. Those who can listen well build trust, foster good relationships, and solve problems faster. If you can uncover issues and deal with them appropriately, you will be much more effective in all of your interactions with others.

LASER has also given me a confidence that I can handle whatever it is that life throws at me. Through practicing the techniques of calm openness, I know that I won't be knocked over when the hard times come.

When I was in college, I played rugby. One of the things my coach taught me has stayed with me all these years. People often think that the way to keep yourself from falling down when you get tackled is to build up your leg muscles, but that's wrong. In fact, the way to keep from getting knocked to the ground is to build up your stomach muscles, your core. That's the part of you that keeps you balanced, and a strong core can keep you upright even when something strong and heavy flies at you.

For those for whom tackling is not a helpful analogy, yoga might work. Balance poses, like the tree pose, rely on our having a solid and stable core, as well as a steady focus on a fixed point. I love balance poses because there is no better way to force the extraneous out of my brain. If my mind wanders, I fall over. I am forced to keep my thoughts clear and my eyes fixed on a given point. My entire body held aloft by one foot, with arms open and wide, I can hold only three things in my head: my strong core, my point of focus, and my breath.

I think of LASER as a way to reinforce my core. It gives me the strength and focus to remain stable and upright when life throws something heavy at me. Because of LASER, I have the confidence to face any situation. I know that it's not my job to change whatever hard thing someone is experiencing, but I can listen, acknowledge what he's going through, give him information and tools or resources, and I can return—both to him and to myself.

I know that these steps will help him, no matter what he's facing. A positive response to a story of trauma can impact the person's physical and emotional healing, making him more likely to access the help he needs and recover from the traumatic event. It also shows him respect and helps to restore a sense of dignity and autonomy that he may have lost through all that he's experienced. I know that while I cannot always see the impact of my support, an affirming and supportive response makes a difference over the long term in his healing. I can trust that I've done what I can to help him.

LASER also helps our organizations. When we respond appropriately to difficult issues in the workplace, we make it more likely that those hard issues will surface, so they can be addressed. The issues already exist—domestic violence, sexual harassment and assault, bias, addiction, fraud and other financial problems, mental and physical health issues are all common in the workplace. If we work with people, we are working with people in trauma. Having a less supportive response when the issues arise does not make them go away, it merely drives them underground, where they affect our organizations in lost productivity, absenteeism, attrition, and more. As Justice Louis D. Brandeis noted, "Sunlight is said to be the best of disinfectants; electric light the most efficient policeman." Giving others the space to bring their issues to the surface, instead of forcing them to fester, creates the ability to address those issues in a humane and efficient way. A positive response—a LASER response—does the same thing for the organization that it does between individuals: it builds trust, and it helps those in pain to get on the path to healing.

Organizations need strong cores too. Things will fly at our organizations, and sometimes they'll be powerful and heavy. An environmental disaster. A data breach. A gunman in the lobby. If our organizations are already versed in handling hard issues because we've been practicing—we've faced illness, harassment, and bullying with openness and calm—then we will be able to handle the bigger stuff too. Change is the only constant, as they say. LASER allows us to be nimble enough to weather those changes, whatever they are and whenever they come.

This is also, incidentally, how we change the world. The percentage of those who suffer from anxiety is increasing at an alarming pace, particularly among young people.[2] Suicide rates have gone up more than 30 percent in recent years.[3] In 2020, as our world faced a global pandemic alongside widespread protests of racism, we saw in stark relief how much our actions affect the people around us and how essential it is that we learn to listen to those in trauma.

If we can practice calm and openness in response to turmoil, we can diffuse tension and help the people who need it. What those who have been brave enough to speak out deserve is active listening. Acknowledgment. The information they crave. Access to services. And ongoing support. They deserve the focus to remain on them long enough to get them onto the path to recovery, and to have someone equip them for the journey.

Life is messy, yes. We can't get through it alone. Fortunately, we don't have to.

# Acknowledgments

I n the words of Joan Didion, "I don't know what I think until I write it down." Writing this book has given me the opportunity to explore issues at the core of my passion—how to support one another in this beautiful and broken world. I will be forever grateful to my agent, Maryann Karinch of the Rudy Agency, and my editor, Sara Kendrick of HarperCollins Leadership, for believing in the message of this book and trusting me to deliver it. Thank you, as well, to Jeff Farr, Beth Metrick, and Zoe Kaplan, who have edited with skill, precision, and kindness.

A lawyer by training, I have benefited enormously from the work and guidance of psychologists in preparing this book. Fortunately, I have found in general that psychologists are a wise and generous group (not necessarily so for lawyers). I want to express my gratitude in particular to Dr. Jim Hopper, Dr. Chris Wilson, Dr. Anne DePrince, Dr. Stephanie Kendall, and Meghan Riordan Jarvis, MA and LICSW. Any errors in the book are due solely to my failures in comprehension and expression, and not to their considerable efforts to educate and enlighten me.

One of my greatest treasures in life is my community of friends. Throughout the writing of this book, friends have listened, encouraged, inspired, and shared their stories with me. I wish to thank in particular Samantha Brunick, Laurie Cameron, Anjali Chaturvedi, Kate Connelly, Mila Drumke, Joey Fortuna, Rosanna Lopez King, Faye McCray, Pippa Shulman, Laurie Sternberg, and Jelahn Stewart. Special thanks are due to Leilani Schweitzer, both for allowing me to share her story here and for her wisdom that shaped my thinking on apologies and healing. Finally, I must extend my gratitude to Sejal Patel. It was in conversations with Sejal that the idea for this book first materialized and the framework for it solidified.

I wish to thank Smith College and the University of Virginia School of Law for sharpening my thinking, honing my writing, and giving me lifelong friendships. The libraries and librarians of American University, where I teach, have been instrumental to my research on this book. The Executive Women's Leadership Program at George Washington University, led by Leslie Grossman, helped clarify my message and goals.

I am so grateful for my time at the Justice Department, where I was surrounded every day by bright, dedicated public servants who strive to do justice. I am especially grateful to the victim witness personnel in the United States Attorneys' Offices, from whom I learned so much about supporting those in need. I also wish to thank the shelters where I volunteered early in my career, including Necessities/Necesidades (now Safe Passage) in Northampton, Massachusetts; the DC Rape Crisis Center and the House of Ruth in Washington, DC; the Shelter for Help in Emergency in Charlottesville, Virginia; and Battered Women's Alternatives (now STAND!) in Contra Costa County, California. I am so glad I had the opportunity to work with these incredible organizations and the communities they serve.

I would be remiss not to acknowledge the contribution of Barry's Tea to my pleasure and clarity of thought during early morning writing sessions.

Finally, my family. My wife, Susan Baker Manning, and our three children are the central support, inspiration, and delight of my life. Josh Sherwin can always make me laugh and always make me think. Janice Lloyd gives me the strength to try things that seem impossible. And to my mother, Anita Manning: your courage, grace, and compassion have been the model I strive to emulate every day.

# Notes

## CHAPTER 1

1. Interviews with Benton [a pseudonym] on February 5, 2020, and in April 2019. Some identifying details about the city have been changed.

## CHAPTER 2

1. Roy Maurer, "When Domestic Violence Comes to Work," SHRM Online (citing study by Corporate Alliance to End Domestic Violence).
2. April Fulton, "In Texas and Beyond, Mass Shootings Have Roots in Domestic Violence," NPR, November 7, 2017 (noting that while perpetrators of domestic violence are responsible for 10 percent of gun violence overall, they are responsible for 54 percent of mass shootings); Hilary Brueck and Shana Lebowitz, "The Men behind the US's Deadliest Mass Shootings Have Domestic Violence—Not Mental Illness—in Common," *Business Insider*, August 15, 2019 (finding that nine of the ten deadliest mass shootings in US history were perpetrated by men who had committed or threatened violence against intimate partners or female family members).
3. Roy Maurer, "When Domestic Violence Comes to Work," SHRM Online.
4. Rhitu Chatterjee, "A New Survey Finds 81 Percent of Women Have Experienced Sexual Harassment," NPR, February 21, 2018 (reporting results of online survey conducted by Stop Street Harassment in January 2018).
5. Rachael Rettner, "6 Ways Sexual Harassment Damages Women's Health," *LiveScience*, November 9, 2011; Elyse Shaw, Ariane Hegewisch, and Cynthia Hess, "Sexual Harassment and Assault at Work: Understanding the Costs," Institute for Women's Policy Research, available at https://iwpr.org/publications/sexual-harassment-work-cost/.
6. Shaw, Hegewisch, and Hess, "Sexual Harassment and Assault at Work." For those who have been on teams with sexual harassment, the reason for this will be clear—gossip, suspicion, jealousy, and fear cloud all work activity.
7. Joe Davidson, "#MeToo, #NoMore, now #HowMuch? What Is the Cost of Sexual Harassment?" *Washington Post*, June 8, 2018, available at https://www.washingtonpost.com/news/powerpost/wp/2018/06/08/senators-continue-search-for-sexual-harassment-economic-data-after-labor-dept-refuses-to-help/.
8. Shaw, Hegewisch, and Hess, "Sexual Harassment and Assault at Work" (noting that the cost of employee turnover averages 16 to 20 percent of the employee's annual salary, up to 213 percent of the salary for experienced managerial and professional staff).
9. Desta Fekedulegn, Toni Alterman, et al, "Prevalence of Workplace Discrimination and Mistreatment in a National Sample of Older U.S. Workers: The REGARDS Cohort Study," *SSM-Population Health* 8 (2019): 100444.
10. Fekedulegn and Alterman, "Prevalence of Workplace Discrimination."

11. Kathy Caprino, "New Data Reveals the Hard Cost of Bias and How to Disrupt It," *Forbes*, October 26, 2017.

12. Sharon G. Smith et al., "National Intimate Partner and Sexual Violence Survey: 2015 Data Brief," available at https://www.cdc.gov/violenceprevention/datasources/nisvs /2015NISVSdatabrief.html.

13. "Sexual Violence in the Workplace," National Sexual Violence Resource Center, 2013, citing E. M. Ellis, B. M. Atkeson, and K. S. Calhoun, "An Assessment of Long-Term Reaction to Rape," *Journal of Abnormal Psychology* 90, 263–66.

14. Rochelle F. Hanson, et al, "The Impact of Crime Victimization on Quality of Life," *Journal of Traumatic Stress* 23, no. 2 (April 2010): 191 (citing Ellis, Atkeson, and Calhoun, "Long-Term Reaction to Rape").

15. John Wihbey, "Rates of Fraud, Identity Theft and Scams across the 50 States: FTC Data," Journalists' Resource, a website by Harvard's Shorenstein Center on Media, Politics, and Public Policy, March 5, 2015.

16. According to a study by Javelin Strategy and Research, reported by the Insurance Information Institute, available at https://www.iii.org/fact-statistic/facts-statistics-identity -theft-and-cybercrime.

17. Paul Stratt, "5 Ways Identity Theft Can Wreak Havoc," *Experian blog*, available at https:// www.experian.com/blogs/ask-experian/5-ways-identity-theft-can-wreak-havoc/.

18. Kelli B. Grant, "What to Do When a Personal Identity Theft Becomes a Professional Problem," CNBC, January 8, 2019, available at https://www.cnbc.com/2019/01/07 /how-identity-theft-causes-problems-at-work.html.

19. Grant, "What to Do When a Personal Identity Theft Becomes a Professional Problem."

20. Centers for Disease Control and Prevention, National Center for Chronic Disease Control and Health Promotion, "About Chronic Diseases," October 23, 2019, available at https://www.cdc.gov/chronicdisease/about/index.htm.

21. Lynn Feinberg and Rita Choula, "Understanding the Impact of Family Caregiving at Work," AARP Policy Institute Fact Sheet 271 (October 2012), available at https:// www.aarp.org/content/dam/aarp/research/public_policy_institute/ltc/2012 /understanding-impact-family-caregiving-work-AARP-ppi-ltc.pdf.

22. Feinberg and Choula, "Caregiving at Work."

23. National Safety Council Safety Topics, "Assault at Work," available at https://injuryfacts .nsc.org/work/safety-topics/assault/.

24. Jana Kasperkevic, "The costly aftermath of a workplace shooting," NPR's Marketplace, June 26, 2019, available at https://www.marketplace.org/2019/06/26/workplace-violence -shooting-aftermath-costly/.

25. Donna M. Gates, Gordon L. Gillespie, and Paul Succop, "Violence against Nurses and Its Effect on Stress and Productivity," CNE Series, *Nursing Economic$* 29, no. 2 (March/ April 2011).

26. Gates, Gillespie, and Succop, "Violence against Nurses."

27. Audrey Carlson, et al., "#MeToo Brought Down 201 Powerful Men. Nearly Half Their Replacements Are Women," *New York Times*, October 29, 2018, available at https:// www.nytimes.com/interactive/2018/10/23/us/metoo-replacements.html. See also Riley Griffin, Hannah Recht, and Jeff Green, "#MeToo: One Year Later," *Bloomberg*, October 5, 2018, available at https://www.bloomberg.com/graphics/2018-me-too-anniversary/ (detailing 425 public accusations of sexual misconduct).

28. Yohana Desta, "After Months-Long Death Rattles, the Weinstein Company Is Officially Kaput," *Vanity Fair,* July 16, 2018, available at https://www.vanityfair.com/hollywood /2018/07/the-weinstein-company-lantern-entertainment.

29. Samantha Cooney, "Companies Are Losing Millions after #MeToo Allegations Like Kate Upton's Claim against Guess' Paul Marciano," *Time*, February 2, 2018.

30. Cooney, "Companies Are Losing Millions."

31. Cooney, "Companies Are Losing Millions."
32. Mariel Padilla, "Judge Signals Approval of U.S.C.'s $215 Million Settlement with Ex-Gynecologist's Patients," *New York Times*, January 7, 2020.
33. C. Ashley Fulmer and Michele J. Gelfand, "At What Level (and in Whom) We Trust: Trust across Multiple Organizational Levels," *Journal of Management* 38, no. 4 (July 2012): 1168 (collecting study results; citations omitted).
34. Stephen M. R. Covey and Douglas R. Conant, "The Connection between Employee Trust and Financial Performance," *Harvard Business Review*, July 18, 2016.
35. Covey and Conant, "Trust and Financial Performance."
36. Paul J. Zak, "The Neuroscience of Trust," *Harvard Business Review* (January/February 2017).
37. MonaPatel, "Workplace Harassment: Why Women Don't Speak Up," *Forbes*, October 30, 2018.
38. Not her real name.
39. Jim Hopper, "Repeat Rape by College Men," available at https://www.jimhopper.com/repeat-rape-by-college-men/.

## CHAPTER 3

1. Throughout this book, I use the terms "victim," "survivor," and "person in trauma" interchangeably. From my own background in criminal justice, I tend to use the word "victim," as it is a legal term of art that denotes entitlement to certain rights and services. Many prefer the word "survivor," however, as it focuses on recovery and on the person's response to the wrong—victims are acted upon; survivors act. Finally, "person in trauma" is more all-encompassing. Some of those who are in trauma may not be victims or survivors of the actions of another and may not feel that either term is accurately applied to them. Whenever possible, it is best to use the term that the person prefers. See, for example, Kate Harding, "I've Been Told I'm a Survivor, Not a Victim. But What's Wrong with Being a Victim?" *Time*, February 27, 2020.

## CHAPTER 4

1. Brains are incredibly complex and individual, and our reactions to trauma can vary greatly due to life experience, predisposition, and impairments like the use of drugs or alcohol. The information contained in this chapter is a broad overview, but understand that trauma may appear differently in some individuals and some circumstances.
2. Amy F. T. Arnsten, "Stress Signaling Pathways That Impair Prefrontal Cortex Structure and Function," *Nature Review Neuroscience* 10, no. 6 (June 2009): 410–22; Claire Bates, "Blanking Out: How Stress Can Shut Down the Command Centre in the Brain," *Daily Mail*, April 10, 2012 (updated April 11, 2010), available at https://www.dailymail.co.uk/sciencetech/article-2127686/How-stress-shut-command-centre-brain.html; Nancy Moyer, "Amygdala Hijack: When Emotion Takes Over," Healthline.com, available at https://www.healthline.com/health/stress/amygdala-hijack#overview.
3. John Mark Taylor, "Mirror Neurons after a Quarter Century: New Light, New Cracks," Harvard University Graduate School of Arts and Sciences, *Science in the News* blog, July 25, 2016, available at http://sitn.hms.harvard.edu/flash/2016/mirror-neurons-quarter-century-new-light-new-cracks/. The underlying study is Giuseppe Di Pellegrino et al, "Understanding Motor Events: A Neurophysiological Study," *Experimental Brain Research* 91 (1992): 176–80, available at 10.1007/BF00230027.
4. Netherlands Institute for Neuroscience - KNAW, "I feel you: Emotional mirror neurons found in the rat," ScienceDaily, available at https://www.sciencedaily.com/releases/2019/04/190411115239.htm. The cited study is Maria Carrillo et al, "Emotional Mirror Neurons in the Rat's Anterior Cingulate Cortex," *Current Biology*, 2019; DOI: 10.1016/j.cub.2019.03.024.

5. Stacey Colino, "Are You Catching Other People's Emotions?" *U.S. News and World Report,* January 20, 2016, available at https://health.usnews.com/health-news/health-wellness/articles/2016-01-20/are-you-catching-other-peoples-emotions.
6. "Could 'Mirror Neurons' Explain Brain Mechanisms of Empathy?" *Medical News Today,* citing Maria Carrillo, et al, "Emotional Mirror Neurons in the Rat's Anterior Cingulate Cortex, *Current Biology,* 2019; DOI: 10.1016/j.cub.2019.03.024.
7. Igor Riecansky and Claus Lamm, "The Role of Sensorimotor Processes in Pain Empathy," *Brain Topography* 32, no. 6 (November 2019): 965–76.
8. "Could 'Mirror Neurons' Explain Brain Mechanisms of Empathy?" *Medical News Today,* citing Maria Carrillo et al, "Emotional Mirror Neurons in the Rat's Anterior Cingulate Cortex," *Current Biology,* 2019; DOI: 10.1016/j.cub.2019.03.024.
9. Veronika Engert et al, "Cortisol Increase in Empathic Stress Is Modulated by Emotional Closeness and Observation Modality," *Psychoneuroendocrinology* 45 (July 2014): 192–201.
10. For a fun example of this, search online for videos of "when someone tells you to run prank."
11. Stephanie Kirby, "Fight Flight Freeze: How to Recognize It and What to Do When it Happens," *Better Help,* November 7, 2019, available at https://www.betterhelp.com/advice/trauma/fight-flight-freeze-how-to-recognize-it-and-what-to-do-when-it-happens/.

## CHAPTER 5

1. See "50 Obstacles to Leaving," National Domestic Violence Hotline, June 10, 2013, available at https://www.thehotline.org/2013/06/10/50-obstacles-to-leaving-1-10/.
2. This reasoning continues to this day. Family court judges usually do not consider a history of domestic violence relevant when making custody and visitation determinations. Even worse, as batterers often have access to more money and thus better attorneys, they use the court system to continue their abuse by, for example, persuading the court that the typically erratic behavior of domestic violence victims (such as frequent moves and a wariness about sharing their whereabouts) is evidence that they are unstable parents. According to a 2012 study by the American Judges Association, "Batterers have been able to convince authorities that the victim is unfit or undeserving of sole custody in approximately 70% of challenged cases." See Natalie Pattillo, "For Abuse Survivors, Custody Remains a Means by Which Their Abusers Can Retain Control," *Pacific Standard,* March 29, 2018, available at https://psmag.com/social-justice abuse-survivors-custody-battl. See also Samantha Schmidt, "'A Gendered Trap': When Mothers Allege Child Abuse by Fathers, the Mothers Often Lose Custody," *Washington Post,* July 29, 2019, relying on Joan S. Meier and Sean Dickson, "Mapping Gender: Shedding Empirical Light on Family Courts' Treatment of Cases Involving Abuse and Alienation," *Law & Inequality* 35 (2017): 311 (finding that when mothers alleged abuse, including child abuse, they lost custody more than twice as often as did fathers who alleged abuse).
3. Kathryn A. Branch and Tara N. Richards, "The Effects of Receiving a Rape Disclosure: College Friends' Story," *Violence Against Women* 19, no. 5: 658–70, available at https://doi.org/10.1177/1077801213490509. See also Chapter 45 on compassion fatigue.

## CHAPTER 6

1. *From Madness to Hope: The 12-Year War in El Salvador,* Report of the Commission on the Truth for El Salvador, Art. II. The Mandate, recounted in Aaron Lazare, *On Apology* (Oxford: Oxford University Press, 2005).
2. Aaron Lazare, *On Apology* (Oxford: Oxford University Press, 2005), 45, citing Martha Minow, *Between Vengeance and Forgiveness* (Boston: Beacon Press, 1998).

3. Gina Roberts-Grey, "Keeping Secrets Can Be Hazardous to Your Health," *Forbes*, October 24, 2013.
4. Courtney E. Ahrens, Janna Stansell, and Amy Jennings, "To Tell or Not to Tell: The Impact of Disclosure on Sexual Assault Survivors' Recovery," *Violence and Victims* 25, no. 5 (May 2010): 631–48.
5. Hayley Robinson, Paul Jarrett, et al, "The Effects of Expressive Writing before or after Punch Biopsy on Wound Healing," *Brain, Behavior, and Immunity* 61 (March 2017): 217–27.
6. Leila Levinson, "Can the Simple Act of Storytelling Help Them to Heal?" *HuffPost*, November 9, 2011.
7. Rita Charon, "Narrative Medicine: A Model for Empathy, Reflection, Profession, and Trust," *JAMA*, October 17, 2001.
8. Barbara Stahura, "Writing to Heal: The Veterans' Writing Project," BrainLine, July 10, 2013.
9. Chanel Miller, *Know My Name: A Memoir* (New York: Viking, 2019).
10. "Larry Nassar Case: The 156 Women Who Confronted a Predator," BBC News, January 25, 2018.
11. Liz Brody, "The Army of Women Who Took Down Larry Nassar," *Glamour*, October 30, 2018.
12. Sonia Moghe and Lauren del Valle, "Larry Nassar's Abuse Victims, in Their Own Words," CNN, January 17, 2018.
13. Leslie Goldman, "Why Sharing Your Personal Story Can Offer Real Health Benefits," on Oprah.com.
14. Lazare, *On Apology*, citing Alan Riding, "Nazis' Human Cargo Now Haunts French Railway," *New York Times*, March 20, 2003. See also Alan Riding, "Rail Ride to Death: Jew Seeks One Euro, Wants French Firm to Express Remorse," *Gazette* (Montreal, Quebec), March 21, 2003. Though Schaechter lost his suit on statute of limitations grounds, he succeeded in bringing attention to the role of the French railroad in supporting Nazi atrocities. See Alan Riding, "Suit Accusing French Railways of Holocaust Role Is Thrown Out," *New York Times*, May 15, 2003.

## CHAPTER 7

1. Here's an exercise you can try with a friend or family member. One of you should describe a recent experience that was exciting or fun while the other listens with hard eyes for thirty seconds. Make intense eye contact. Don't nod. Don't smile. Don't react to what you're hearing. When Wilson does this exercise with groups he trains, the reactions are almost always the same. "It felt like they weren't listening." "I didn't think they cared." "I wanted to stop talking." "It was like nothing I said mattered."
2. CDC's National Intimate Partner and Sexual Violence Survey (2015), at 8 & 9, 4.
3. Having a cell phone on the table reduces the quality of an in-person conversation, even when no one touches the phone. Shalini Misra, Lulu Cheng, Jamie Genevie, and Miao Yuan, "The iPhone Effect: The Quality of In-Person Social Interactions in the Presence of Mobile Devices," *Environment and Behavior* 48, no. 2 (February 2016): 275–98. doi:10.1177/0013916514539755.

## CHAPTER 8

1. Ralph G. Nichols and Leonard A. Stevens, "Listening to People," *Harvard Business Review*, September 1957.
2. Douglas Heingartner, "Now Hear This, Quickly," *New York Times*, October 2, 2003.
3. Jack Zenger and Joseph Folkman, "What Great Listeners Actually Do," *Harvard Business Review*, July 14, 2016.

4.  Elizabeth Kiehner, "When over Half of Communication Comes through Body Language, Do You Understand How You Interact with Others When You're Not in the Room?" *Inc.*, August 28, 2018, citing Albert Mehrabian, *Silent Messages* (1971).

## CHAPTER 9

1.  Interview of Meghan Riordan Jarvis, MA and LICSW, January 14, 2020.

## CHAPTER 10

1.  Ronald P. Fisher and R. Edward Geiselman, *Memory-Enhancing Techniques for Investigative Interviewing: The Cognitive Interview* (Springfield, IL: Charles C. Thomas Publisher, 1992), 26 (emphasis in original).
2.  Rhitu Chatterjee, "How Trauma Affects Memory: Scientists Weigh in on the Kavanaugh Hearing," NPR, September 28, 2018, available at https://www.npr.org/sections/health-shots/2018/09/28/652524372/how-trauma-affects-memory-scientists-weigh-in-on-the-kavanaugh-hearing. The article notes that facts related to the fear response become encoded and specific, while those on the periphery are vaguer. As an example, a store clerk who is robbed might have a very clear memory of the gun aimed at him but be unclear on whether the gunman wore glasses. His attention, of course, was focused on the gun and not on the person holding it.

## CHAPTER 13

1.  Janice Gassam Asare, "Overcoming the Angry Black Woman Stereotype," *Forbes*, May 31, 2019. See also Brittany Cooper, *Eloquent Rage* (New York: St. Martin's Press, 2018).

## CHAPTER 14

1.  Substance Abuse and Mental Health Services Administration, "Key substance use and mental health indicators in the United States: Results from the 2018 National Survey on Drug Use and Health," Center for Behavioral Health Statistics and Quality, Substance Abuse and Mental Health Services Administration, HHS Publication no. PEP19-5068, NSDUH Series H-54 (2019): 47–48. Available at https://www.samhsa.gov/data/.
2.  Madelyn S. Gould, et al, "Evaluating iatrogenic risk of youth suicide screening programs," *JAMA* 293, no. 13 (April 6, 2005).
3.  However, people who say, "Maybe I'd jump off a bridge or something," may be minimizing to protect you or themselves from knowing how suicidal they are, so we can never write off any suicidal thoughts. It's important in all cases to keep talking and to get the person to appropriate resources.
4.  From the National Institute of Mental Health website on "Suicide in America: Frequently Asked Questions," accessed on February 3, 2020. Available at https://www.nimh.nih.gov/health/publications/suicide-faq/index.shtml#pub3.
5.  The Federal Communications Commissions has designated 988 to be the national suicide prevention lifeline beginning in July 2022.
6.  EAP and other counseling services are discussed in more detail in Chapter Thirty-Seven.
7.  William Wan, "More Americans Are Killing Themselves at Work," *Washington Post*, January 9, 2020, recounting a Bureau of Labor Statistics report that shows an 11 percent increase in the number of suicides in 2018 over the previous year—the highest number of suicides since the Bureau began tracking the data twenty-six years previously.
8.  Available at https://theactionalliance.org/resource/managers-guide-suicide-postvention-workplace-10-action-steps-dealing-aftermath-suicide.

9. The Federal Child Abuse Prevention and Treatment Act requires each state to have rules governing the mandated reporting of child abuse and neglect. To see the rules in your state, do an online search for your state plus "mandatory reporting," or see the information collected by the Department of Health and Human Services' Children's Bureau at https://www.childwelfare.gov/pubPDFs/manda.pdf#Page=1&view=Fit.

10. There is a list of elder abuse mandatory reporting laws by state here: https://www.stetson.edu/law/academics/elder/home/statutory-updates.php. The list also delineates where and how to make a report.

11. You can access information on where to report child abuse in your state here: https://www.childwelfare.gov/topics/responding/reporting/how/.

## CHAPTER 16

1. All names and some details have been changed.

## CHAPTER 17

1. Lindsay M. Orchowski, Amy S. Untied, and Christine A. Gidycz, "Social Reactions to Disclosure of Sexual Victimization and Adjustment Among Survivors of Sexual Assault," *Journal of Interpersonal Violence* 28, no. 10 (2013): 2005–23.

2. Orchowski, Untied, Gidycz, "Social Reactions"; Mark Relyea and Sarah E. Ullman, "Unsupported or Turned Against: Understanding How Two Types of Negative Social Reactions to Sexual Assault Relate to Postassault Outcomes," *Psychology of Women Quarterly* 39, no. 1 (2015): 37–52.

3. See Anne P. DePrince, Courtney Welton-Mitchell, and Tejaswinhi Srinivas, "Longitudinal Predictors of Women's Experiences of Social Reactions Following Intimate Partner Abuse," *Journal of Interpersonal Violence* 29 (February 2014): 2509–23.

4. Interview with Anne DePrince, February 19, 2020.

5. Carly Parnitzke Smith and Jennifer J. Freyd, "Dangerous Safe Havens: Institutional Betrayal Exacerbates Sexual Trauma," *Journal of Traumatic Stress* 26 (February 2013): 119–24; Jennifer J. Freyd, Bridget Klest, and Carolyn B. Allard, "Betrayal Trauma: Relationship to Physical Health, Psychological Distress, and a Written Disclosure Intervention," *Journal of Trauma & Dissociation* 6, no. 3 (2005).

## CHAPTER 18

1. Alan Goldman, "The Deadly Inappropriate Smile," *Psychology Today*, November 17, 2016.
2. Goldman, "Inappropriate Smile."

## CHAPTER 20

1. Stephen Dubner, *Freakonomics* Podcast Episode 344, "Who Decides How Much a Life Is Worth?" (August 8, 2018) (Interview with Kenneth Feinberg), available at http://freakonomics.com/podcast/kenneth-feinberg/.

2. Tweet of Christa Brown, @ChristaBrown777, February 10, 2020.

## CHAPTER 21

1. See Alison Wood Brooks, Hengchen Dai, and Maurice E. Schweitzer, "I'm Sorry about the Rain! Superfluous Apologies Demonstrate Empathic Concern and Increase Trust," *Social Psychology and Personality Science* 5, no. 4 (May 2014): 467–74, available at https://www.hbs.edu/faculty/Publication%20Files/Brooks%20Dai%20Schweitzer%202013_d2f61dc9-ec1b-485d-a815-2cf25746de50.pdf.

## CHAPTER 22

1. Melvin J. Lerner, "Evaluation of Performance as a Function of Performer's Reward and Attractiveness," *Journal of Personality and Social Psychology* 1, no. 4 (1965): 355–60.
2. Melvin J. Lerner and Carolyn H. Simmons, "Observer's Reaction to the 'Innocent Victim': Compassion or Rejection?" *Journal of Personality and Social Psychology* 4, no. 2 (1966): 203–10. See also Jonah Lehrer, "A Just World," *Atlantic*, September 1, 2009 (noting that subjects judged the woman more harshly the less they were told she had gotten paid for participating in the experiment, seemingly to bring about "a more appropriate fit between her fate and her character").
3. Orchowski, Untied, Gidycz, "Social Reactions."
4. *This American Life* episode 682: Ten Sessions, available at https://www.thisamericanlife.org/682/transcript.
5. Megan Twohey and Jodi Kantor, "This Is the Toughest Question Facing Harvey Weinstein's Jury," *New York Times*, February 7, 2020.
6. Ella Torres, "Why Assault Victims Stay in Touch with Attackers, in Light of Weinstein Defense," ABC News, January 23, 2020.
7. Torres, "Why Assault Victims Stay in Touch."
8. Joan Cook and Jessi Gold, "'Friendly' Emails Are Not Evidence Harvey Weinstein Did Nothing Wrong," *Newsweek*, January 9, 2020.
9. Torres, "Why Assault Victims Stay in Touch."
10. National Institute of Justice, "Most Victims Know Their Attacker," September 30, 2008, nij.ojp.gov: https://nij.ojp.gov/topics/articles/most-victims-know-their-attacker.

## CHAPTER 25

1. Dennis Thompson, "Fewer Medical Malpractice Lawsuits Succeed, but Payouts Are Up," CBS News, March 28, 2017.
2. Lazare, *On Apology*, citing Pumla Gobodo-Madikizela, *A Human Being Died That Night: A South African Story of Forgiveness* (Boston: Houghton-Mifflin, 2003), 130.
3. Interviews with Leilani Schweitzer on October 9, 2019, and February 7, 2020.

## CHAPTER 26

1. Richard C. Boothman et al., "A Better Approach to Medical Malpractice Claims? The University of Michigan Experience," *Journal of Health and Life Sciences Law* 125 (January 2009): 144. See also Lee S. Goldsmith, "An MD Attorney Reveals: Top 5 Reasons Patients Sue Doctors," *Medscape*, October 23, 2018.

## CHAPTER 28

1. Blog of Leilani Schweitzer, "Compassion & Disclosure = The Standard of Care (Medicine X)," September 7, 2014.

## CHAPTER 29

1. Suze Wilson, "Three Reasons Why Jacinda Ardern's Coronavirus Response Has Been a Masterclass in Crisis Leadership," *Conversation*, April 5, 2020, available at https://theconversation.com/three-reasons-why-jacinda-arderns-coronavirus-response-has-been-a-masterclass-in-crisis-leadership-135541.
2. Eleanor Ainge Roy, "Jacinda Ardern Hits Poll High as National Urged to Get Over Bridges," *Guardian*, May 18, 2020, available at https://www.theguardian.com/world/2020/may/19/jacinda-ardern-poll-high-popularity-national-simon-bridges-new-zealand-covid-19.

## CHAPTER 30

1. Lazare, *On Apology*, 37–40.

## CHAPTER 33

1. Brooks, Dai, and Schweitzer, "I'm Sorry About the Rain!"
2. Interview with Leilani Schweitzer, February 7, 2020.
3. Maurice E. Schweitzer, Alison Wood Brooks, and Adam Galinsky, "The Organizational Apology," *Harvard Business Review*, September 2015.
4. Maev Kennedy and Jamie Grierson, "PwC issues apology after Oscars best picture envelope mistake," *Guardian*, February 27, 2017.
5. Statement from PricewaterhouseCoopers, February 27, 2017, available at https://www.oscars.org/news/statement-pricewaterhousecoopers.
6. Peter Page, "Mark Zuckerberg Doesn't Seem Very Sorry or Very Forgiven," *Entrepreneur*, March 22, 2018, available at https://www.entrepreneur.com/article/310865.
7. Sarah Green Carmichael, "Research: For a Corporate Apology to Work, the CEO Should Look Sad," *Harvard Business Review*, August 24, 2015, available at https://hbr.org/2015/08/research-for-a-corporate-apology-to-work-the-ceo-should-look-sad. See also Erin O'Hara O'Connor, "Organizational Apologies: BP as a Case Study," *Vanderbilt Law Review* 64, no. 6 (November 2011): 1957, 1961, finding that despite extensive efforts to express regret and take responsibility for the Deep Horizon oil spill, "BP created the impression that its statements were insincere through a series of public images and comments that dampened and counteracted the effectiveness of its apologies."
8. Bonnie Ackerman, "You Had Me at 'I'm Sorry': The Impact of Physicians' Apologies on Medical Malpractice Litigation," *National Law Review*, November 6, 2018.
9. F. R. LeCraw et al., "Changes in Liability Claims, Costs, and Resolution Times Following the Introduction of a Communication-and-Resolution Program in Tennessee," *Journal of Patient Safety and Risk Management* 23, no. 1 (2018): 13–18. See also Ackerman, "You Had Me at 'I'm Sorry'"; Jennifer K. Robbennolt, "Apologies and Medical Error," *Clinical Orthopedics and Related Research* 467, no. 2 (February 2009): 376–82, finding that apologies "can decrease blame, decrease anger, increase trust, and improve relationships" and "have the potential to decrease the risk of a medical malpractice lawsuit and can help settle claims by patients."
   A 2019 article published in the *Stanford Law Review* concluded, in contrast, that apology laws, which bar evidence of an apology by a doctor or hospital in a subsequent lawsuit, actually increased both the number of suits filed and the award or settlement amount. (Benjamin J. McMichael, R. Lawrence Van Horn, and W. Kip Viscusi, "'Sorry' Is Never Enough: How State Apology Laws Fail to Reduce Medical Malpractice Liability Risk," *Stanford Law Review* 41 [February 2019]: 341.) The study's authors, though, fault poor training of doctors in how to apologize and the laws themselves for protecting only the statement of apology and not the statements accepting responsibility, without which an apology can ring hollow. ("'Sorry' Is Never Enough," 386–89.) "[T]he limited protection offered by apology laws may actually encourage, rather than discourage, malpractice claims because patients may not be able to obtain all of the information they desire about their injuries from statements involving only partial apologies." ("'Sorry' Is Never Enough," 89, citing Anna C. Mastroianni et al, "The Flaws in State 'Apology' and 'Disclosure' Laws Dilute Their Intended Impact on Malpractice Suits," *Health Affairs* 29 [2010]: 1611, 1616.)
10. Richard C. Boothman et al, "A Better Approach to Medical Malpractice Claims? The University of Michigan Experience," *Journal of Health and Life Sciences Law* 125 (January 2009): 144. See also Jathan Janove, "A 'Sorry' Strategy," SHRM, March 1, 2006, discussing apologies in medical malpractice, airline, and employment disputes.
11. Boothman, "A Better Approach," 133.

## CHAPTER 34

1. Laura Shin, "'Someone Had Taken Over My Life': An Identity Theft Victim's Story," *Forbes*, November 18, 2014.
2. "Self defence: Identity-theft monitoring," *Economist* 424, no. 9058 (September 16, 2017).

## CHAPTER 35

1. Christopher Wilson, Kimberly Lonsway, and Joanne Archambault, "Understanding the Neurobiology of Trauma and Implications for Interviewing Victims," November 2016, available at https://www.evawintl.org/Library/DocumentLibraryHandler .ashx?id=842.
2. If you are interested in learning more about why victims of domestic violence stay with their abusers, there are compelling victim stories recounted in "The Most Dangerous Time: Five Women Tell Their Stories of Leaving an Abusive Relationship," *Guardian* (Australia) (interviews by Melissa Davey).
3. The exception to this rule is when the person is a danger to himself or others, as set forth in Chapter Fourteen.

## CHAPTER 37

1. Keith Matos, Ellen Galinsky, and James T. Bond, National Study of Employers, SHRM (2017).
2. Matos, Galinsky, and Bond.
3. HR Q&As, "General: What Is an Employee Assistance Program (EAP)?" SHRM.
4. Alia Hoyt, "Why Hardly Anyone Uses Employee Assistance Programs," How Stuff Works, August 22, 2017.
5. Hoyt, "Why Hardly Anyone." For ideas on how to increase usage, see Joanna Sammer, "Solving the EAP Underuse Puzzle: Employee Assistance Programs (EAPs) Can't Work if Employees Don't Use Them," SHRM, August 8, 2014.
6. 211 is widely, but not universally, available. If it is not available in your area, use 311 instead.
7. For more on 211's services, see https://www.fcc.gov/consumers/guides/dial-211-essential -community-services.
8. The Federal Communications Commission has designated 988 to direct callers to the National Suicide Prevention Lifeline beginning in July 2022. For more information on suicide in the workplace, see Chapter Fourteen .

## CHAPTER 38

1. Not her real name.

## CHAPTER 39

1. For the locations that do not have 211, use 311 instead.

## CHAPTER 40

1. Brigid Finn, "Ending on a High Note: Adding a Better End to Effortful Study," *Journal of Experimental Psychology: Learning, Memory, and Cognition* 36, no. 6 (2010): 1548–53. doi:10.1037/a0020605, available at https://www.ncbi.nlm.nih.gov/pmc/articles /PMC2970645/. The water was 14 degrees Celsius, or 57.2 degrees Fahrenheit, then was raised to 15 degrees Celsius, or 59 degrees Fahrenheit.

2.    Id. Similar experiments had the same results with loud sounds, aversive movie clips, pressure from a vise, and painful medical procedures.

3.    Amy M. Do et al, "Evaluations of Pleasurable Experiences: The Peak-End Rule," *Psychonomic Bulletin & Review* 15, no. 1 (2008): 96–98.

## CHAPTER 44

1.    Jerome A. Motto and Alan G. Bostrom, "A Randomized Controlled Trial of Postcrisis Suicide Prevention," *Psychiatric Services* 52, no. 7 (June 2001).

## CHAPTER 45

1.    Kelsey's Story, as told on the website for the foundation started by her family, https://kelseysarmy.org/#about-us.

2.    "The Teen Who Never Came Home from the Store: Local Mysteries," Investigation Discovery, May 4, 2019, available at https://www.youtube.com/watch?v=4Kr3LiOBT9U.

3.    "The Teen Who Never Came Home."

4.    "The Teen Who Never Came Home."

5.    Prepared Testimony of Missey Smith, Mother of Kelsey Smith, in Support of Nev. S.B. 268, May 6, 2013, available at https://www.leg.state.nv.us/Session/77th2013/Exhibits/Assembly/CL/ACL1052E.pdf.

6.    Transcript of video prepared for Office for Victims of Crime, 2019 Ronald Wilson Reagan Public Policy Award to Missey Smith of The Kelsey Smith Foundation, Overland Park, Kansas, available at https://ovcncvrw.ncjrs.gov/Awards/AwardGallery/gallerysearch.html.

7.    Information obtained from the Kelsey Smith Foundation website at https://kelseysarmy.org/#ks-act and https://kelseysarmy.org/#about-us.

8.    Transcript of video prepared for Office for Victims of Crime, 2019 Ronald Wilson Reagan Public Policy Award to Missey Smith of The Kelsey Smith Foundation, Overland Park, Kansas, available at https://ovcncvrw.ncjrs.gov/Awards/AwardGallery/gallerysearch.html.

9.    Rachel A. Cohen, "Some Trauma Really Is Unspeakable. So These Women Are Sewing Their Stories, Instead," *Washington Post,* November 27, 2019.

10.   Interview with Leilani Schweitzer, February 7, 2020.

11.   Office for Victims of Crime, 2019 Special Courage Award to Shari Kastein, available at https://ovcncvrw.ncjrs.gov/Awards/AwardGallery/gallerysearch.html.

12.   Aaron Reuben, "When PTSD Is Contagious: Therapists and Other People Who Help Victims of Trauma May Become Traumatized Themselves," *Atlantic,* December 14, 2015.

13.   Reuben, "When PTSD Is Contagious."

14.   Andrew P. Levin and Scott Greisberg, "Vicarious Trauma in Attorneys," 24 Pace L. Rev. 245 (2003).

15.   U.S. Department of Health and Human Services, Administration for Children and Families Fact Sheet on Secondary Traumatic Stress, available at https://www.acf.hhs.gov/trauma-toolkit/secondary-traumatic-stress.

16.   Department of Health and Human Services Fact Sheet on Secondary Traumatic Stress.

17.   Robert A. Emmons & Michael E. McCullough, "Counting Blessings vs. Burdens: An Experimental Investigation of Gratitude and Subjective Well-Being in Daily Life," *Journal of Personality and Social Psychology* 84, no. 2 (2003): 377–89, available at https://greatergood.berkeley.edu/images/application_uploads/Emmons-CountingBlessings.pdf. In one study, those who wrote about things they were grateful for every week for ten weeks felt better about their lives, were more optimistic, had fewer health complaints, and spent more time exercising than control groups who counted hassles or neutral life events.

## CHAPTER 46

1. Jena McGregor, "Why Sexual Harassment Training Doesn't Stop Harassment," *Washington Post*, November 17, 2017.
2. Sara Sutton, "Why Every Boss Should Consider Offering Flexible Work Opportunities to Their Employees," *Inc.*, October 16, 2018.
3. Roy Maurer, "When Domestic Violence Comes to Work," SHRM, October 16, 2018.
4. Not her real name.

## CHAPTER 47

1. Marianna Pogosyan, "In Helping Others, You Help Yourself," *Psychology Today*, May 30, 2018, noting that those who helped others with their problems experienced greater self-regulation, lower risk of depression, and an overall improvement in well-being.
2. Jamie Ducharme, "A Lot of Americans Are More Anxious Than They Were Last Year, a New Poll Says," *Time*, May 8, 2018, citing a poll by the American Psychological Association that found that nearly 40 percent of Americans reported that they were more anxious than they'd been the year before; Amy Ellis Nutt, "Why Kids and Teens May Face Far More Anxiety These Days," *Washington Post*, May 10, 2018, citing the National Survey of Children's Health, which found that rates of anxiety among children ages six to seventeen increased by 20 percent from 2007–2012.
3. Kirsten Weir, "Worrying Trends in U.S. Suicide Rates," *American Psychological Association, Monitor on Psychology* 50, no. 3 (March 2019), noting that the suicide rate increased by 33 percent from 1999 to 2017.

# Index

# About the Author

**Katharine Manning** has been an advocate, counselor, and legal advisor on victim issues for more than twenty-five years. As a senior attorney advisor with the Justice Department, for fifteen years she guided the department through its response to victims in high-profile cases like the Boston Marathon bombing, the Pulse nightclub and South Carolina church shootings, the violence in Charlottesville, Bernie Madoff, and the case against Olympic Gymnastics team doctor Larry Nassar. Now president of Blackbird, Manning helps organizations prepare for and respond to the challenges they face involving employees and members of the public in crisis. She has trained thousands of individuals on compliance with their responsibilities to victims, and she teaches a course on victim rights at American University. Prior to her government service, Manning was an attorney in private practice representing Fortune 500 companies in class action, insurance, and media cases. She is a graduate of Smith College and the University of Virginia School of Law.